Praise for Aaron Shepard's *Readers on Stage*

At last! If you've been looking for a complete resource for teaching and using readers theatre, look no further. From scripts, to implementation strategies, to materials for workshops, *Readers on Stage* has it all. Aaron Shepard draws upon decades of work to provide a practical, well-organized, and reader-friendly book. Don't miss it!

Dr. Suzanne Barchers
Author, *Readers Theatre for Beginning Readers*, and publisher, Storycart Press

Aaron Shepard skillfully envelops us in the wonderful world of readers theatre. His new book melds the how-to-do-it with engaging, entertaining scripts. This is a welcome contribution to the field.

Dr. Shirlee Sloyer
Professor, Hofstra University, and author, *From the Page to the Stage*

For more than a decade, Aaron Shepard has been recognized nationally as an innovative, skilled, highly successful practitioner of readers theatre with emphasis on support of literature and reading, especially for teachers at elementary and middle-school levels. His latest book gives concise, clear, and practical tips for scriptmaking and staging, along with useful scripts and

Dr. William Ada
Director, Institu

Readers on Stage solves the instructor's problem of ᵢ
readers' theater for the drama student. Even a person experienced in theater has much to learn from Aaron Shepard's insightful book.

Dr. Rebecca Saunders
Professor of Drama, Lesley University

Aaron Shepard has written a breezy, easy guide to help any teacher begin exploring the exciting and imaginative worlds of readers theatre. Every element needed for getting started is here: philosophies, methodologies, helpful tips, and sample scripts. What are the benefits? A child's widened understanding of good stories, enhanced imaginative response, heightened spatial awareness, increased cooperation, and greater love of literature can all result from the program presented in this generous book. Highly recommended!

James Floss
Lecturer, Communication Department, Humboldt State University

Also by Aaron Shepard

Professional Resources

Stories on Stage: Scripts for Reader's Theater
Folktales on Stage: Scripts for Reader's Theater
The Business of Writing for Children
Tell a Tale! (forthcoming)

Picture Books

King o' the Cats
The Princess Mouse: A Tale of Finland
Master Man: A Tall Tale of Nigeria
Lady White Snake: A Tale From Chinese Opera
The Sea King's Daughter: A Russian Legend
The Baker's Dozen: A Saint Nicholas Tale
The Magic Brocade: A Tale of China
Forty Fortunes: A Tale of Iran
The Crystal Heart: A Vietnamese Legend
Master Maid: A Tale of Norway
The Maiden of Northland: A Hero Tale of Finland
The Gifts of Wali Dad: A Tale of India and Pakistan
The Enchanted Storks: A Tale of Bagdad
The Legend of Slappy Hooper: An American Tall Tale
The Legend of Lightning Larry
Savitri: A Tale of Ancient India
Two-Eyes (forthcoming)

Chapter Books, Novels, and Collections

Timothy Tolliver and the Bully Basher (forthcoming)
Monkey: A Superhero Tale of China (forthcoming)
Mad, Magic, and Marvelous: Classic Tales of the World (forthcoming)

Readers

ON STAGE

Resources for Reader's Theater (or Readers Theatre),
With Tips, Play Scripts, and Worksheets

Aaron Shepard

Shepard Publications
Los Angeles

Author Online!

For more reader's theater, visit
Aaron Shepard's RT Page at

www.aaronshep.com/rt

ISBN-13:   978-0-938497-21-9
ISBN-10:   0-938497-21-9

Library of Congress Control Number: 2003099521
Library of Congress subject headings:
Readers' theater
Children's plays

"The Legend of Lightning Larry" was published as a script first in *Stories on Stage,* H. W. Wilson, New York, 1993. "The Baker's Dozen" was published as a script first in *Folktales on Stage,* Shepard Publications, Los Angeles, 2004.

Part 2, "RT Tips," was published first as *Readers on Stage: Tips for Reader's Theater,* Shepard Publications, Pacific Grove, California, 1997. "Tips on Scripting" appeared first as the appendix of *Stories on Stage,* H. W. Wilson, New York, 1993. "Tips on Staging" appeared first as an article in *The Reading Teacher,* October 1994. "Tips on Reading" appeared first as an article in *The California Reader,* Winter 1995.

Most of the scripting worksheets in Part 3 were published first as an independent set by Shepard Publications, Pacific Grove, California, 1997.

1.0

Contents—Short

Introduction 9

Part 1 ~ RT Scripts 11

 The Legend of Lightning Larry 13
 Peddler Polly and the Story Stealer 23
 The Baker's Dozen 33

Part 2 ~ RT Tips 39

 Tips on Scripting 41
 Tips on Staging 47
 Tips on Reading 54

Part 3 ~ An RT Workshop 57

 Sample Materials List 61
 Sample Outlines 63
 Notes and Handouts 67
 Scripting Worksheets 73

Part 4 ~ Other RT Resources 99

 Books and Articles 100
 Online Resources 102
 Suppliers 103
 Training 104

Index 107

Contents—Long

Introduction   9

    What Is RT? (And How Do You Really Spell It?)   9

    About This Book   10

    About the Web Site   10

Part 1 ~ RT Scripts   11

The Legend of Lightning Larry   13

PREVIEW: A cowboy with a huge smile, a gun that shoots bolts of light, and a hankering for lemonade takes on Evil-Eye McNeevil's outlaw gang.

GENRE: Fables (original), tall tales, humor   READERS: 22 or more
CULTURE: American (Western frontier)   READER AGES: 7–12
THEME: Peacemaking   LENGTH: 8 minutes

Peddler Polly and the Story Stealer   23

PREVIEW: The storytellers of Taletown are mysteriously losing their stories, while a stranger sells "storyboxes" in the town square.

GENRE: Fables (original), humor   READERS: 13 or more
CULTURE: ——   READER AGES: 9–12
THEME: Television   LENGTH: 10 minutes

The Baker's Dozen   33
A Saint Nicholas Tale

PREVIEW: Van Amsterdam, the baker, is as honest as he can be—but he may have something left to learn.

GENRE: Legends, St. Nicholas tales   READERS: 6 or more
CULTURE: American (Dutch colonial)   READER AGES: 8–13
THEME: Generosity   LENGTH: 6 minutes

Part 2 ~ RT Tips   39

Tips on Scripting   41
Script Roles   41
Cuts and Changes   42
Narration   43
Script Format   43
Team Scripting   44

Tips on Staging   47
Equipment   48
Script Handling   48
The Set   49
Reader Movement   49
Mime and Sound Effects   50
Focus   52
Beginnings and Endings   53

Tips on Reading   54
Preparing   54
Rehearsing   55
Performing   56

Part 3 ~ An RT Workshop   57

Sample Materials List   61

Sample Outlines   63
1 hour   64
1½ hours   65
3½ hours   66

Notes and Handouts   67
From Story to Script   68
Sample Script Page   69
From Script to Stage   70
Tips for Readers   71
RT Resources   72

Part 3 ~ An RT Workshop (continued)

Scripting Worksheets   73

Master Man   74

The Sea King's Daughter   75

King o' the Cats   76

The Princess Mouse   77

The Baker's Dozen   78

Savitri: A Tale of Ancient India   79

The Magic Brocade   80

The Enchanted Storks   81

Master Maid   82

Forty Fortunes   83

The Legend of Slappy Hooper   84

The Gifts of Wali Dad   85

More Than a Match   86

Peddler Polly and the Story Stealer   87

Kings for Breakfast   88

The Boy Who Wanted the Willies   89

The Magic of Mushkil Gusha   90

The Millionaire Miser   91

The Lady of Stavoren   92

The Hidden One   93

The Four Puppets   94

The Story Spirits   95

The Wicked Girl   96

Lars, My Lad!   97

I Know What I Know   98

Part 4 ~ Other RT Resources   99

Books and Articles   100

Online Resources   102

Suppliers   103

Training   104

Index   107

Introduction

What Is RT? (And How Do You *Really* Spell It?)

Reader's theater is minimal theater in support of literature and reading. There are many styles of reader's theater, but nearly all share these features:

- Narration serves as the framework of dramatic presentation.
- No full stage sets. If used at all, sets are simple and suggestive.
- No full costumes. If used at all, costumes are partial and suggestive, or neutral and uniform.
- No full memorization. Scripts are used openly in performance.

Reader's theater was developed as an efficient and effective way to present literature in dramatic form. Today as well, most scripts are literary adaptations, though others are original dramatic works.

Popular first in colleges and universities, reader's theater has now moved to earlier education, where it is seen as a key tool for creating interest and skill in reading. Young people love to do it, and they give it their all—more so because it's a team effort, and they don't want to let down their friends! Repeated readings bring fluency, and if a script is based on an available book, kids want to read that too. What's more, reader's theater is a relatively simple activity for the teacher, with no required setup other than making copies of scripts.

Reader's theater has been found effective not only for language arts but for social studies as well. Performing stories based on another culture is one of the best ways for students to become interested in and familiar with that culture.

As to how to spell it, there's no one right way, so take your pick! All the following have been used:

- reader's theater
- readers' theater
- readers theater
- reader's theatre
- readers' theatre
- readers theatre

That's why it's sometimes easier to call it RT!

About This Book

Readers on Stage is a collection of resources for scripting, directing, and teaching reader's theater, primarily to ages 8 or 9 and up. It draws on my five years of professional experience in reader's theater as a performer and a director, as well as many more years of scripting, leading workshops, and hosting the most popular reader's theater destination on the Web.

Part 1 offers three sample scripts to learn from and enjoy. Part 2 provides detailed tips on scripting, staging, and dramatic reading. Part 3 supplies everything else you need to start with reader's theater in the classroom or library or to conduct your own reader's theater workshop for adults. And Part 4 gives listings of additional resources. All materials may be freely copied and shared for any noncommercial purpose (except some may not be posted online without permission, as noted).

About the Web Site

For updates, many more scripts, and other resources, please visit Aaron Shepard's RT Page at www.aaronshep.com/rt. And while you're visiting, be sure to sign up for my email bulletin. There's always more to come!

Aaron Shepard

Part 1 ~ RT Scripts

I always start my reader's theater workshops by having the group perform a script—so why not start this book in a similar way? Here then are three scripts adapted from my own stories: "The Legend of Lightning Larry," "Peddler Polly and the Story Stealer," and "The Baker's Dozen." Among them, they cover a wide range in the number of readers required—so if you're giving a workshop or a lesson, you should be able to find a script here to fit the size of your group.

The scripts may be freely copied, shared, and performed for any noncommercial purpose, except they may not be posted online without permission. Feel free to edit the scripts to serve the needs of your own readers.

At the beginning of each script, you'll find notation on genre, culture of origin or setting, theme, number of readers, suggested reader ages, and approximate reading time, as well as a brief description of the story.

Also at the beginning of each script is a list of roles. A reader, of course, can be assigned more than one role, as long as only one role is "onstage" at a time. When a script is short on female characters, it's common to cast females in male roles.

Roles listed in parentheses are unscripted, with no assigned speech, and usually optional. These roles can be given to surplus readers if your directing style includes stage movement or if you choose to add speeches or sounds for these readers. In the reader count, unscripted roles are indicated by the phrase "or more."

For more tips on using the scripts, see Part 2. For more scripts, see my books *Stories on Stage* and *Folktales on Stage,* and visit Aaron Shepard's RT Page at www.aaronshep.com/rt.

The Legend of Lightning Larry

By Aaron Shepard

Adapted for reader's theater by the author, from his picture book published by Scribners, New York, 1993

> For more reader's theater, visit Aaron Shepard's RT Page at
> **www.aaronshep.com/rt**

PREVIEW: A cowboy with a huge smile, a gun that shoots bolts of light, and a hankering for lemonade takes on Evil-Eye McNeevil's outlaw gang.

GENRE: Fables (original), tall tales, humor   READERS: 22 or more
CULTURE: American (Western frontier)   READER AGES: 7–12
THEME: Peacemaking   LENGTH: 8 minutes

ROLES: Citizens 1–8, Lightning Larry, Crooked Curt, Evil-Eye McNeevil, Dismal Dan, Devilish Dick, Dreadful Dave, Stinky Steve, Sickening Sid, Raunchy Ralph, Grimy Greg, Creepy Cal, Moldy Mike, Lousy Luke, Gruesome Gus, (Other Citizens), (Musicians), (Bartender), (Bank Teller)

NOTES: CITIZENS serve as narrators. For best effect, place CITIZENS 1 to 4 at far left, and 5 to 8 at far right, as seen from the audience. If possible, all readers should speak with a Western drawl. For special features, visit www.aaronshep.com/extras.

CITIZEN 1: Well, you've heard about gunfighting good guys like Wild Bill Hickok and Wyatt Earp.

CITIZEN 8: But we'll tell you a name that strikes even greater fear into the hearts of bad men everywhere.

ALL (except LARRY): Lightning Larry!

CITIZEN 2: We'll never forget the day Larry rode into our little town of Brimstone and walked into the Cottonmouth Saloon. He strode up to the bar and smiled straight at the bartender.

LIGHTNING LARRY: *(with a huge smile)* Lemonade, please!

CITIZEN 7: Every head in the place turned to look.

CITIZEN 3: Now, standing next to Larry at the bar was Crooked Curt.

CITIZEN 6: Curt was one of a band of rustlers and thieves that had been terrorizing our town, led by a ferocious outlaw named Evil-Eye McNeevil.

CITIZEN 4: Curt was wearing the usual outlaw scowl.

CITIZEN 5: Larry turned to him and smiled.

LIGHTNING LARRY: Mighty big frown you got there, mister!

CROOKED CURT: What's it to *you?*

LIGHTNING LARRY: Well, maybe I could help remove it!

CROOKED CURT: I'd like to see you try!

CITIZEN 1: The rest of us got out of the way real fast.

CITIZEN 8: The bartender ducked behind the bar.

CITIZEN 2: Larry and Curt moved about ten paces from each other, hands at the ready.

CITIZEN 7: Larry was still smiling.

CITIZEN 3: Curt moved first. But he only just cleared his gun from its holster before Larry aimed and fired.

LIGHTNING LARRY: *Zing!*

CITIZEN 6: There was no bang and no bullet. Just a little bolt of light that hit Curt right in the heart.

CITIZEN 4: Curt just stood there, his eyes wide with surprise. Then he dropped his gun, and a huge grin spread over his face.

CITIZEN 5: He rushed up to Larry and pumped his hand.

CROOKED CURT: I'm mighty glad to know you, stranger! The drinks are on me. Lemonade for everyone!

* * *

CITIZEN 1: When Evil-Eye McNeevil and his outlaw gang heard that Crooked Curt had gone straight, they shuddered right down to their boots.

CITIZEN 8: Most any outlaw would rather die than smile!

CITIZEN 2: Evil-Eye's men were shook up, but they weren't about to let on.

CITIZEN 7: The very next day,

DISMAL DAN: Dismal Dan!

DEVILISH DICK: Devilish Dick!

DREADFUL DAVE: And Dreadful Dave!

CITIZEN 7: rode into Brimstone, yelling like crazy men and shooting wild.

DAN, DICK, & DAVE: *(hoot and holler, prance, wave guns and shoot)*

CITIZEN 3: Windows shattered

CITIZEN 6: and citizens scattered.

CITIZEN 4: Then Lightning Larry showed up. He never warned them.

CITIZEN 5: Never even stopped smiling.

CITIZEN 1: Just shot three little bolts of light.

LIGHTNING LARRY: *Zing! Zing! Zing!*

DAN, DICK, & DAVE: *(stop and fall when hit)*

CITIZEN 8: Hit those outlaws right in the heart.

CITIZEN 2: Larry's shots knocked the outlaws to the ground. They lay there trying to figure out what had hit them. Then they got up and looked around.

DISMAL DAN: Looks like we did some damage, boys.

CITIZEN 7: . . . said Dismal Dan.

DEVILISH DICK: Hope nobody got hurt!

CITIZEN 3: . . . said Devilish Dick.

DREADFUL DAVE: We'd better get to work and fix this place up.

CITIZEN 6: . . . said Dreadful Dave.

CITIZEN 4: They spent the rest of the day replacing windows and apologizing to everyone who'd listen.

CITIZEN 5: Then for good measure, they picked up all the trash in the street.

* * *

CITIZEN 1: Evil-Eye McNeevil had lost three more of his meanest men,

CITIZEN 8: and he was furious!

CITIZEN 2: He decided to do something *really* nasty.

CITIZEN 7: The next day,

STINKY STEVE: Stinky Steve!

SICKENING SID: And Sickening Sid!

CITIZEN 7: walked into the 79th National Savings and Loan with guns in hand.

CITIZEN 3: They wore masks,

CITIZEN 6: but everyone knew who they were—from the smell.

STINKY STEVE: Stick up your hands.

CITIZEN 4: . . . said Stinky Steve.

SICKENING SID: Give us all the money in your vault.

CITIZEN 5: . . . ordered Sickening Sid.

CITIZEN 1: They were just backing out the door with the money bags, when Lightning Larry strolled by.

CITIZEN 8: Didn't even slow his step.

CITIZEN 2: Just shot those bandits in the back.

LIGHTNING LARRY: *Zing! Zing!*

CITIZEN 7: Went right through to the heart.

CITIZEN 3: The puzzled outlaws stopped and looked at each other.

STINKY STEVE: Seems a shame to steal the money of hardworking cowboys.

SICKENING SID: Wouldn't want to make their lives any harder.

CITIZEN 6: They holstered their guns and walked back to the teller.

CITIZEN 4: They plunked the money bags down on the counter.

SICKENING SID: Now, you keep that money safe.

CITIZEN 5: Then they pulled out their wallets and opened up accounts.

* * *

CITIZEN 1: That was the last straw for Evil-Eye McNeevil. It was time for a showdown!

CITIZEN 8: The next day at high noon, Larry was sipping lemonade at the Cottonmouth Saloon. Evil-Eye burst through the doors and stamped up to him.

EVIL-EYE McNEEVIL: I'm Evil-Eye McNeevil!

LIGHTNING LARRY: *(with a huge smile)* Hello, Evil-Eye! Can I buy you a lemonade?

EVIL-EYE McNEEVIL: This town ain't big enough for the both of us.

LIGHTNING LARRY: Seems pretty spacious to me!

EVIL-EYE McNEEVIL: I'll be waiting for you down by the Okey-Dokey Corral.

CITIZEN 8: And Evil-Eye stamped out.

CITIZEN 2: Larry finished his lemonade and walked out onto Main Street.

CITIZEN 7: Evil-Eye was waiting for him. But Evil-Eye wasn't alone.

CITIZEN 3: There on either side of him were

RAUNCHY RALPH: Raunchy Ralph!

GRIMY GREG: Grimy Greg!

CREEPY CAL: Creepy Cal!

MOLDY MIKE: Moldy Mike!

LOUSY LUKE: Lousy Luke!

GRUESOME GUS: And Gruesome Gus!

CITIZEN 6: And not a one of them looked friendly.

LIGHTNING LARRY: Nice day for a stroll!

CITIZEN 4: . . . called Larry.

EVIL-EYE McNEEVIL: Draw!

CITIZEN 5: . . . said Evil-Eye.

CITIZEN 1: All of us citizens of Brimstone were lining Main Street to see what would happen.

CITIZEN 8: Larry was still smiling, but we knew even Larry couldn't outshoot all those outlaws together.

CITIZEN 2: Just then a voice came from the Cottonmouth Saloon.

CROOKED CURT: Like some help, Larry?

LIGHTNING LARRY: Wouldn't mind it!

CITIZEN 7: Out stepped . . . Crooked Curt! And right behind him were Dismal Dan, Devilish Dick, Dreadful Dave, Stinky Steve, and Sickening Sid.

CITIZEN 3: They all took places beside Larry.

CROOKED CURT: Hello, Evil-Eye!

CITIZEN 6: . . . called Curt.

EVIL-EYE McNEEVIL: Traitors!

CITIZEN 4: . . . yelled Evil-Eye.

LIGHTNING LARRY: Draw!

CITIZEN 5: . . . said Larry, with a smile.

CITIZEN 1: Evil-Eye and his men drew their guns,

CITIZEN 8: but Larry and his friends were an eye-blink quicker.

CITIZEN 2: Their guns fired seven little bolts of light.

LARRY & FRIENDS: *Zing!*

CITIZEN 7: Hit those outlaws right in the you-know-what.

EVIL-EYE McNEEVIL: YIPPEE!

CITIZEN 3: . . . yelled Evil-Eye.

CITIZEN 6: He shot in the air.

EVIL-EYE McNEEVIL: *Zing!*

CITIZEN 4: There was no bang and no bullet.

CITIZEN 5: Just a little bolt of light.

LIGHTNING LARRY: All right, men! Let's clean up this town once and for all!

LARRY & ALL OUTLAWS: *(shoot at all others) Zing! Zing! Zing! . . .*

CITIZEN 1: And before we could duck for cover,

CITIZEN 8: Larry and Evil-Eye and the others

CITIZEN 2: turned their guns on the *rest* of us.

CITIZEN 7: Bolts of light flew everywhere.

CITIZEN 3: *No* one was spared—

CITIZEN 6: not a man,

CITIZEN 4: woman,

CITIZEN 5: or child!

ALL (except LARRY): YIPPEE!

CITIZEN 1: You never saw such a happy crowd!

CITIZEN 8: We all rushed around

CITIZEN 2: and pumped each other's hands

CITIZEN 7: and hugged each other.

CITIZEN 3: Then the musicians got out instruments and we had dancing too. Main Street was one huge party,

CITIZEN 6: all the rest of that day

CITIZEN 4: and on through the night.

CITIZEN 5: We never drank so much lemonade in all our days!

* * *

CITIZEN 1: With all the commotion, only a few of us saw Larry ride into the sunset.

CITIZEN 8: Can't say where he went.

CITIZEN 2: Can't say what he's doing now.

CITIZEN 7: But we bet he still aims for the heart.

ALL: *(shooting at audience)* Zing!

Peddler Polly and the Story Stealer

By Aaron Shepard

Adapted for reader's theater by the author

> For more reader's theater, visit Aaron Shepard's RT Page at
> **www.aaronshep.com/rt**

PREVIEW: The storytellers of Taletown are mysteriously losing their stories, while a stranger sells "storyboxes" in the town square.

GENRE: Fables (original), humor
CULTURE: ——
THEME: Television

READERS: 13 or more
READER AGES: 9–12
LENGTH: 10 minutes

ROLES: Narrators 1–4, Peddler Polly, Penny, Spellbinder, Crowd 1–3, Bertha Bigwig, Milton Marbles, Jack, (Other Crowd), (Audience), (Pied Piper), (Children), (Giant), (Pegasus)

NOTES: For best effect, place NARRATORS 1 and 2 at far left, and 3 and 4 at far right, as seen from the audience. For special features, visit www.aaronshep.com/extras.

NARRATOR 1:

> **PEDDLER POLLY**
> **Goods Bought Here**
> **and Sold There**

NARRATOR 4: That was the sign on Peddler Polly's cart as her horse pulled her up Main Street. Peddler Polly looked around and smiled.

PEDDLER POLLY: I'm sure glad to be back in Taletown. Imagine—a town where everyone tells stories!

NARRATOR 2: Peddler Polly parked at the town square. Over on Town Hall she saw a notice:

NARRATOR 3:

```
┌─────────────────────────────────────┐
│                                      │
│          STORY SWAP TODAY            │
│            Bring a story             │
│         (if you still know one)      │
│                                      │
└─────────────────────────────────────┘
```

PEDDLER POLLY: *(puzzled)* If you still know one?

PENNY: *(sadly)* Hello, Peddler Polly.

NARRATOR 1: . . . came a sad little girl's voice.

PEDDLER POLLY: Well, it's my old friend Penny! Do you have a good story for me? I'll gladly trade for something from my cart.

NARRATOR 4: Penny sobbed and sniffed.

PENNY: I don't have any stories at all! Hardly anyone in Taletown does. We're all losing our stories!

PEDDLER POLLY: Losing your stories? Whatever do you mean?

PENNY: We start to tell a story, and then it's gone! We can't remember it anymore. Come to the Story Swap this afternoon and see.

SPELLBINDER: *(loudly)* Ladies and gentlemen, boys and girls . . .

NARRATOR 2: Another cart had parked on the square. Its sign said,

NARRATOR 3:

DR. SEBASTIAN SPELLBINDER
Entertainment Paraphernalia

NARRATOR 1: In the cart stood a man with a topcoat, top hat, and goatee, surrounded by piles of wooden boxes.

NARRATOR 4: A crowd was gathering before him.

SPELLBINDER: You've heard of a story*teller.* And you've heard of a story*book.* Well, I'm here to show you something finer still: The brand-new, patented Spellbinder Storybox!

PENNY: *(delighted)* Oh, Peddler Polly! He's selling *stories!*

NARRATOR 2: Dr. Spellbinder held up one of the wooden boxes, showing a pane of glass on one side.

NARRATOR 3: He flipped a switch and the glass came to life. Tiny characters moved across the pane, and tiny voices came out.

NARRATOR 1: Someone in the crowd yelled,

CROWD 1: It's "Cinderella"!

NARRATOR 4: Dr. Spellbinder turned a knob, and a different moving picture appeared.

CROWD 2: That's "Puss in Boots"!

NARRATOR 2: He turned the knob again.

CROWD 3: And that's "Sleeping Beauty"!

SPELLBINDER: Never again will you have to ask for a story. And never again will you have to imagine the pictures! Who'll be the first to buy a Spellbinder Storybox?

CROWD 1: I'll take one!

CROWD 2: So will I!

CROWD 3: I'll take two!

NARRATOR 3: Before long, Dr. Spellbinder's cart was empty. The town square was covered with children and grownups, all staring blankly at the little boxes.

PEDDLER POLLY: *(to herself)* I don't like the looks of this.

* * *

NARRATOR 1: When Peddler Polly arrived at the Story Swap that afternoon, Town Hall was packed. The room was buzzing with talk about lost stories and Spellbinder Storyboxes.

NARRATOR 4: Finally, Mayor Bertha Bigwig took the stage. She glanced nervously around her.

BERTHA BIGWIG: Welcome to the Story Swap. It is my honor to tell the first story: "The Pied Piper of Hamlin."

NARRATOR 2: From her seat by an open window, Peddler Polly heard a soft *whirr* and a sucking noise.

BERTHA BIGWIG: Life in the town of Hamlin was pleasant. Or it *would* have been, if not for the . . . the . . .

NARRATOR 3: The mayor turned pale.

BERTHA BIGWIG: I've lost my story!

NARRATOR 1: . . . and she ran from the stage. A horrified murmur rose in the room.

NARRATOR 4: Milton Marbles, the schoolteacher, tried next.

MILTON MARBLES: My story is "Jack and the Beanstalk."

NARRATOR 2: Again Peddler Polly heard the *whirr* and the sucking.

MILTON MARBLES: There was once a poor widow who had an only son named . . . named . . . . Oh no!

NARRATOR 3: He fled the stage in tears.

NARRATOR 1: Next came Penny.

PENNY: This is the myth of "Pegasus."

NARRATOR 4: Peddler Polly heard the noises once more.

PENNY: A long time ago in Greece, there was a horse called Pegasus. This horse was special because . . . because . . . because . . .

BERTHA BIGWIG: Stop the Swap! We can't afford to lose any more stories. It's the end of storytelling in Taletown!

NARRATOR 2: As excited talk filled the room, Peddler Polly thought she heard a cackle out the window.

NARRATOR 3: She looked and saw a man with a topcoat and top hat hurry away from the building. He carried a large wooden box covered with switches, knobs, and dials, with a long hose attached to it.

PEDDLER POLLY: It's Dr. Spellbinder! I'd better look into this.

NARRATOR 1: Peddler Polly hastened from the hall. She followed Dr. Spellbinder from a distance as he left the town and made his way into the hills.

NARRATOR 4: At last Dr. Spellbinder disappeared through the mouth of a cave. Peddler Polly followed him in and stopped in astonishment. The huge cave was filled with mechanisms and contraptions, all of them noisily pulling or pushing or pulsing or pounding.

NARRATOR 2: Dr. Spellbinder stood at a workbench covered with Storyboxes and other strange devices. He set down the big box he was carrying and patted it fondly.

SPELLBINDER: Three more stories to put in my Storyboxes! And all thanks to my brilliant invention, the Spellbinder Story Sucker. Soon I'll steal all the stories in the world! Then *everyone* will need a Storybox, and I'll be rich, *rich,* RICH.

PEDDLER POLLY: Not if *I* can help it!

SPELLBINDER: *(gasps)* Peddler Polly! What are *you* doing here?

PEDDLER POLLY: Putting an end to your evil plans, Spellbinder!

SPELLBINDER: You'll never stop me, Peddler Polly!

NARRATOR 3: Then Dr. Spellbinder grabbed the Story Sucker and sprinted from the cave.

NARRATOR 1: Down the hill sped Dr. Spellbinder, while Peddler Polly puffed in pursuit. Without the Story Sucker, Peddler Polly was faster.

SPELLBINDER: *(yelling back)* You won't catch me so easily.

NARRATOR 4: He lifted the lid on the Story Sucker and reached in.

SPELLBINDER: See how you like *this* story, Peddler Polly.

NARRATOR 2: He threw something behind him. There was a flash of light, and out of nowhere a huge crowd of children appeared, coming uphill toward Peddler Polly. They were led by a man in a many-colored costume, playing on a pipe.

PEDDLER POLLY: Well, I'll be!

NARRATOR 3: Peddler Polly pushed past the startled man and pressed through the crowd of mesmerized children.

PEDDLER POLLY: It's a catchy tune, kids, but I wouldn't follow a pied piper!

NARRATOR 1: Dr. Spellbinder was far ahead, but Peddler Polly ran hard and gained on him.

SPELLBINDER: *(calling back)* One good story deserves another!

NARRATOR 4: . . . and he reached into the Story Sucker. Another flash, and Peddler Polly saw a boy chopping down a gigantic beanstalk. But just then the boy took to his heels, calling,

JACK: Heads up!

NARRATOR 2: Peddler Polly looked up and stopped just in time. A huge man tumbled from the sky and landed with an earth-shaking crash just before her.

PEDDLER POLLY: Didn't know stories could be so dangerous.

NARRATOR 3: Peddler Polly ran around the giant while she waved to the boy and called,

PEDDLER POLLY: Thank you, Jack!

NARRATOR 1: Dr. Spellbinder had vanished behind a hill, and Peddler Polly panted after him. As she rounded the bend, she gasped.

NARRATOR 4: Tied to a landing platform was a lighter-than-air balloon, and Dr. Spellbinder was climbing into the basket.

PEDDLER POLLY: Oh, no! Now he'll get away for sure! Unless . . . unless . . .

SPELLBINDER: It's all over now, Peddler Polly!

NARRATOR 2: Dr. Spellbinder untied the rope and the balloon floated into the air.

SPELLBINDER: But I still have one more story, and it might as well keep you busy.

PEDDLER POLLY: *(to herself)* If it's the one I think it is . . . .

NARRATOR 3: Dr. Spellbinder threw it to the ground. Another flash, and there stood a horse with long and graceful wings.

PEDDLER POLLY: Pegasus!

NARRATOR 1: Peddler Polly ran and leaped onto the horse, and dug in her heels.

NARRATOR 4: The horse flapped its wings smoothly and rose in the air. Up and up it spiraled, until it was flying circles around the dismayed Dr. Spellbinder.

PEDDLER POLLY: Guess you forgot your mythology, Spellbinder. Didn't you know Pegasus was a flying horse?

NARRATOR 2: Peddler Polly rode in close, grabbed Dr. Spellbinder, and flung him across the horse's back.

SPELLBINDER: My Story Sucker!

NARRATOR 3: . . . cried Dr. Spellbinder as the balloon floated away with his invention.

PEDDLER POLLY: I don't guess you'll need it where *you're* going. For a crime like shutting up stories, a judge is sure to shut *you* up—unhappily ever after.

* * *

NARRATOR 1: A few weeks later, when all of Dr. Spellbinder's Storyboxes had been opened and the stories returned to their tellers, the people of Taletown held a big storytelling festival on the town square. Mayor Bigwig announced,

BERTHA BIGWIG: And our special guest for today is Peddler Polly!

ALL (except PEDDLER POLLY and SPELLBINDER): *(not in unison)* Hooray!

PEDDLER POLLY: Well, thanks. And now I'll tell a story called "Peddler Polly and the Story Stealer."

NARRATOR 4: And that's a tale

NARRATOR 2: they'll always tell

NARRATOR 3: in Taletown.

The Baker's Dozen
A Saint Nicholas Tale

Told by Aaron Shepard

Adapted for reader's theater by the author, from his picture book published by Atheneum, New York, 1995

For more reader's theater, visit Aaron Shepard's RT Page at
www.aaronshep.com/rt

PREVIEW: Van Amsterdam, the baker, is as honest as he can be—but he may have something left to learn.

GENRE: Legends, St. Nicholas tales
CULTURE: American (Dutch colonial)
THEME: Generosity

READERS: 6 or more
READER AGES: 8–13
LENGTH: 6 minutes

ROLES: Narrators 1-4, Baker, Woman, (Customers), (Children), (Saint Nicholas)

NOTES: For best effect, place NARRATORS 1 and 2 at far left, and 3 and 4 at far right, as seen from the audience. For special features, visit www.aaronshep.com/extras.

NARRATOR 1: In the Dutch colonial town later known as Albany, New York, there lived a baker, Van Amsterdam, who was as honest as he could be.

NARRATOR 4: Each morning, he checked and balanced his scales, and he took great care to give his customers *exactly* what they paid for—not more, and not less.

NARRATOR 2: Van Amsterdam's shop was always busy, because people trusted him, and because he was a good baker as well. And never was the shop busier than in the days before December 6, when the Dutch celebrate Saint Nicholas Day.

NARRATOR 3: At that time of year, people flocked to the baker's shop to buy his fine Saint Nicholas cookies.

NARRATOR 1: Made of gingerbread, iced in red and white, they looked just like Saint Nicholas as the Dutch know him—

NARRATOR 4: tall and thin, with a high, red bishop's cap, and a long, red bishop's cloak.

NARRATOR 2: One Saint Nicholas Day morning, the baker was just ready for business, when the door of his shop flew open.

NARRATOR 3: In walked an old woman, wrapped in a long black shawl.

WOMAN: I have come for a dozen of your Saint Nicholas cookies.

NARRATOR 1: Taking a tray, Van Amsterdam counted out twelve cookies. He started to wrap them, but the woman reached out and stopped him.

WOMAN: I asked for a dozen. You have given me only twelve.

BAKER: Madam, everyone knows that a dozen *is* twelve.

WOMAN: But *I* say a dozen is *thirteen.* Give me one more.

NARRATOR 4: Van Amsterdam was not a man to bear foolishness.

BAKER: Madam, my customers get *exactly* what they pay for—not more, and not less.

WOMAN: Then you may keep the cookies.

NARRATOR 2: She turned to go, but stopped at the door.

WOMAN: Van Amsterdam! However honest you may be, your heart is small and your fist is tight. *Fall again, mount again, learn how to count again!*

NARRATOR 3: Then she was gone.

NARRATOR 1: From that day, everything went wrong in Van Amsterdam's bakery.

NARRATOR 4: His bread rose too high or not at all.

NARRATOR 2: His pies were sour or too sweet.

NARRATOR 3: His cakes crumbled or were chewy.

NARRATOR 1: His cookies were burnt or doughy.

NARRATOR 4: His customers soon noticed the difference. Before long, most of them were going to other bakers.

BAKER: *(to himself)* That old woman has bewitched me. Is this how my honesty is rewarded?

NARRATOR 2: A year passed.

NARRATOR 3: The baker grew poorer and poorer.

NARRATOR 1: Since he sold little, he baked little, and his shelves were nearly bare. His last few customers slipped away.

NARRATOR 4: Finally, on the day before Saint Nicholas Day, not one customer came to Van Amsterdam's shop.

NARRATOR 2: At day's end, the baker sat alone, staring at his unsold Saint Nicholas cookies.

BAKER: I wish Saint Nicholas could help me now.

NARRATOR 3: Then he closed his shop and went sadly to bed.

NARRATOR 1: That night, the baker had a dream. He was a boy again, one in a crowd of happy children. And there in the midst of them was Saint Nicholas himself.

NARRATOR 4: The bishop's white horse stood beside him, its baskets filled with gifts. Nicholas pulled out one gift after another, and handed them to the children.

NARRATOR 2: But Van Amsterdam noticed something strange. No matter how many presents Nicholas passed out, there were always more to give.

NARRATOR 3: In fact, the more he took from the baskets, the more they seemed to hold.

NARRATOR 1: Then Nicholas handed a gift to Van Amsterdam. It was one of the baker's own Saint Nicholas cookies!

NARRATOR 4: Van Amsterdam looked up to thank him, but it was no longer Saint Nicholas standing there.

NARRATOR 2: Smiling down at him was the old woman with the long black shawl.

NARRATOR 3: Van Amsterdam awoke with a start. Moonlight shone through the half-closed shutters as he lay there, thinking.

BAKER: I always give my customers *exactly* what they pay for—not more, and not less. But why *not* give more?

NARRATOR 1: The next morning, Saint Nicholas Day, the baker rose early.

NARRATOR 4: He mixed his gingerbread dough and rolled it out.

NARRATOR 2: He cut the shapes and baked them.

NARRATOR 3: He iced them in red and white to look just like Saint Nicholas.

NARRATOR 1: And the cookies were as fine as any he had made.

NARRATOR 4: Van Amsterdam had just finished, when the door flew open. In walked the old woman with the long black shawl.

WOMAN: I have come for a dozen of your Saint Nicholas cookies.

NARRATOR 2: In great excitement, Van Amsterdam counted out twelve cookies—

NARRATOR 3: and one more.

BAKER: In this shop, from now on, a dozen is thirteen.

WOMAN: You have learned to count well. You will surely be rewarded.

NARRATOR 1: She paid for the cookies and started out. But as the door swung shut, the baker's eyes seemed to play a trick on him.

NARRATOR 4: He thought he glimpsed the tail end of a long red cloak.

* * *

NARRATOR 2: As the old woman foretold, Van Amsterdam *was* rewarded. When people heard he counted thirteen as a dozen, he had more customers than ever.

NARRATOR 3: In fact, Van Amsterdam grew so wealthy that the other bakers in town began doing the same.

NARRATOR 1: From there, the practice spread to other towns, and at last through all the American colonies.

NARRATOR 4: And this, they say, is how thirteen became the "baker's dozen"—

NARRATOR 2: a custom common for over a century,

NARRATOR 3: and alive in some places to this day.

Part 2 ~ RT Tips

Reader's theater is often defined by what it is not—no memorizing, no props, no costumes, no sets. All this makes reader's theater wonderfully convenient. Still, convenience is not its chief asset.

Like storytelling, reader's theater can create images by suggestion that could never be portrayed realistically on stage. Space and time can be shrunk or stretched, fantastic worlds can be created, marvelous journeys can be enacted. Reader's theater frees the performers and the audience from the physical limitations of conventional theater, letting the imagination soar.

In this section, I'll share with you the "tricks of the trade" for scripting, staging, and dramatic reading. Yes, you can just hand your readers a prepared script, stand them at the front of a room, and let them find their way. But reader's theater can be taken much farther than that, and this section will help you get there.

Enjoy the magic of reader's theater!

Tips on Scripting

Almost any story can be scripted for reader's theater, but some are easier and work better than others. In general, look for stories that are simple and lively, with lots of dialog or action, and with not too many scenes or characters.

Script Roles

First study your chosen story to identify the roles. There are two basic types: *Narrators* tell the story. *Characters* are *in* the story. (In first-person stories, of course, the narrator is also a character.) To help your readers understand the types, you can explain that character parts appear in the story *inside* quotation marks, while narrator parts appear *outside*.

If the group you're working with is small, a story may have more roles than you have readers. In some such cases, a story may simply not be practical for you. But there are often ways to adjust:

• Assign more than one role each to individual readers. But make sure a reader isn't onstage with more than one role at a time!

• "Cut" a character, or combine it with another. Speeches of one character can often be added to those of another.

• Use *character narration* in place of a separate narrator. With this approach, characters read the narrator parts that refer to them or that reflect their point of view. This takes some getting used to, though, and often feels clumsy and unnatural.

Instead of too few readers, you may have more than you need. Here are some ways to involve more of them:

• Use two or more narrators. This is usually a good idea anyway for young readers. For tips on splitting narration, see the "Narration" section below.

• Split characters into two or more. A character can sometimes be converted into a set of characters, with the speaking parts divided among them.

• Assign silent characters. Often stories have minor characters without speaking parts. If your directing style includes stage movement, you can assign these roles to surplus readers. You might also add speeches for them. Crowd scenes can always use extra readers.

Cuts and Changes

Feel free to make cuts and changes in the story that will make your script livelier, simpler to understand, or easier to perform. But be sure to read through and check whether everything in the story still makes sense.

Some authorities on reader's theater will object to even the most minor changes in the author's work. But the author was not writing for performance. If you refrain from making appropriate changes, the author's work may not appear in its best light.

Here are some things you may want to "cut":

• Tag lines. These are the lines that tell us "he said" or "she said." In performance, these seldom do more than break up the flow of the story and trip up the readers. But leave in the ones that give extra information the audience must hear. Also leave in ones that an author has used to build rhythm.

• Long descriptions. Many stories include long sections of narration that slow the action. These can often be shortened or even removed.

• Minor characters or scenes. Cutting these can simplify the stage action or adjust for a small number of readers. Often, important dialog or information can be shifted to another character or scene.

Here are other areas where you might make changes:

• Character splitting or combining. As mentioned earlier, you can combine two or more similar characters into one, or split one into two or more.

• Additional speeches. Some story characters may have no lines, or may be onstage for a long time before they speak. In these cases, you may want to invent brief speeches for them. Also, if the narration tells *about* what a character said, you might convert this into a speech of the character.

• Stage directions. You can often make the script smoother by converting parts of the narration to stage directions for the characters.

• Difficult or obscure language. Though readers should be encouraged to read "up" from their level, some scripts will be much easier to follow—for both readers and audience—if you now and then substitute a simpler word, or split a sentence in two. With foreign stories, you may want to "translate" unfamiliar terms.

• Sexist or demeaning language. Often this can be changed unobtrusively. If not, the story may not be appropriate for young people.

• Aids to reading. You can underline or italicize words that should be stressed, add commas to delineate phrasing, or insert stage directions to indicate the feeling behind speeches.

Narration

In scripts for younger readers, it's usually best to have two or more narrators. Besides creating extra roles, it spreads the responsibility for this very important function. It also helps retain audience interest during long narrative passages.

Splitting the narration can be done as simply or as artfully as you like. The way that is best often depends on how the story was written. Here are some possibilities:

• With two or more narrators, assign them successive paragraphs or half-paragraphs. It's best to adjust paragraph splits so Narrator 1 begins each new scene. This limits the reassignments made necessary by later script changes, such as adding or removing a single narrator speech. To make things more lively, divide your narrators between the ends of the stage, with assigned speeches alternating between the ends.

• With two or more narrators, "bounce" back and forth among them in a way that reflects an author's strong rhythmic structure. This can mean trading off on sentences, or even on phrases.

• Switch to a different narrator with each new scene.

• "Sandwich" the dialog. One narrator speaks both before and after a section of character dialog. Then the next narrator does the same.

• Assign a narrator to each character. Each narrator reads all the lines that refer to their assigned character or that reflect their character's point of view.

• Divide narration between the narrators and the characters themselves. This form of character narration works best if the characters don't actually mention themselves.

In general, the younger the readers, the more narrators you want. Most of my own scripts now get four narrators, and some get as many as eight.

Script Format

Scripts should be neat and easy to read. Readers are supposed to look up often from their scripts, and they will have trouble finding their place again if the page is too crammed with text—*or* if the text is too spread out.

For sample pages with my recommended format, see Figure 1 at the end of this chapter. (Because of the demands of book design, the sample scripts in Part 1 of this book are not quite in ideal format.) Here's what I recommend:

• Large, readable type. I suggest using 12-point Verdana, while 12-point Georgia is also good. Both fonts, designed for reading on the Web, are commonly found on PCs and Macs and are installed automatically with Internet Explorer.

For a smaller typeface like Times, Helvetica, or Arial, 14-point is a better size. Supporting info at the start of the script can be in smaller type to save space.

- Linespacing set at 1½ (halfway between single and double spacing).
- Left margin, 1½ inches. (This is extra-wide to allow for binding and to let readers add stage directions.) Right margin, 1 inch. Top margin, 1 inch, including the header. Bottom margin, ½ inch or more.
- A header at top right with one or two key words from the script title, plus the page number.
- Block paragraph format—no indent, either regular or hanging. A blank line or "space after" following each speech.
- Lines aligned left—not "justified" but with the right margin kept uneven.
- No splitting of speeches—or at least of paragraphs—between one page and the next. The direct way to get this is to insert a page break above any speech that would be split. A better way is to format your paragraphs to "keep lines together" or to "protect" them against splitting, individually or as a paragraph style.
- Clearly distinguishable "role tags." These are the identifiers that tell who says what. Put them in all caps or bold with at least two spaces after, to set them off from other text.
- Clearly distinguishable stage directions. I suggest setting them in parentheses and italics.
- Scene dividers. If there's a sharp break between two scenes instead of a smooth transition, use a row of asterisks or such to signal a pause in reading.
- End marker. Use a line or other marking of your choice to make clear when there are no more pages to read.

Team Scripting

Children working in teams are easily capable of scripting short, simple stories. Here is one approach:

First explain briefly about identifying the types of roles, adjusting for more or fewer readers, and possible cutting. Divide the readers into teams of about four. Assign a one-page story to each team, with each member receiving a copy. (Fables work well.)

The team members read through their story, identify the roles, and divide the roles among themselves. Then they decide who will read what. Each reader underlines his or her own speaking parts—in pencil, to allow changes—and also crosses out anything the whole team agrees to cut. If you wish, these individual copies can later be compiled into a master script in standard format.

Normally, young readers can have a one-page story ready for tryout in about a quarter hour, with practically no adult help. *With* adult help, it can take much longer.

Figure 1a. Sample Script Pages—First Page

Savitri
A Tale of Ancient India

Told by Aaron Shepard

Adapted for reader's theater by the author, from his picture book published by Albert Whitman, Morton Grove, Illinois, 1992

> For more reader's theater, visit Aaron Shepard's RT Page at
> **www.aaronshep.com/rt**

PREVIEW: The princess Savitri must use all her wit and will to save her husband from the god of death.

GENRE: Myths, folktales, legends
CULTURE: Asian Indian (ancient), Hindu
THEME: Heroines, determination

READERS: 11
READER AGES: 9–15
LENGTH: 10 minutes

ROLES: Narrators 1–3, Savitri, Satyavan, Kings 1 & 2, Teacher, Narada, Yama, Goddess

NOTES: This story is probably around 3000 years old. It was first written down about 2000 years ago as part of the *Mahabharata*, India's great national epic. *Savitri* is pronounced "SAH-vit-ree." *Satyavan* is pronounced "SOT-ya-von." *Narada* is pronounced "NAR-a-da." *Yama* is pronounced "YAH-ma," rhyming with "lama." *Mahabharata* is pronounced "MAH-hah-BAR-a-ta." To hear the names, and for other special features, visit www.aaronshep.com/extras.

NARRATOR 1: In India, in the time of legend, there lived a king with many wives but not one child.

NARRATOR 2: Morning and evening for eighteen years, he faced the fire on the sacred altar and prayed for the gift of children.

NARRATOR 3: Finally, a shining goddess rose from the flames.

GODDESS: I am Savitri, child of the Sun. By your prayers, you have won a daughter.

Figure 1b. Sample Script Pages—Second Page

Savitri, 2

NARRATOR 1: Within a year, a daughter came to the king and his favorite wife. He named her Savitri, after the goddess.

NARRATOR 2: Beauty and intelligence were the princess Savitri's, and eyes that shone like the sun. So splendid was she, people thought she herself was a goddess.

NARRATOR 3: Yet when the time came for her to marry, no man asked for her. Her father told her,

KING 1: Weak men turn away from radiance like yours. Go out and find a man worthy of you. Then I will arrange the marriage.

NARRATOR 1: In the company of servants and councilors, Savitri traveled from place to place.

NARRATOR 2: After many days, she came upon a hermitage by a river crossing. Here lived many who had left the towns and cities for a life of prayer and study.

NARRATOR 3: Savitri entered the hall of worship and bowed to the eldest teacher. As they spoke, a young man with shining eyes came into the hall. He guided another man, old and blind.

SAVITRI: *(softly, to the teacher)* Who is that young man?

TEACHER: *(smiling)* That is Prince Satyavan. He guides his father, a king whose realm was conquered. It is well that Satyavan's name means "Son of Truth," for no man is richer in virtue.

NARRATOR 1: When Savitri returned home, she found her father with the holy seer called Narada.

KING 1: Daughter, have you found a man you wish to marry?

SAVITRI: Yes, father. His name is Satyavan.

READERS ON STAGE • 46

Tips on Staging

There are many styles of reader's theater. In the simplest and most traditional:

• Readers are arranged in a row or a semicircle, standing up or sitting on high stools. Typically, narrators are placed at one or both ends, and major characters in the center.

• Scripts can be held in hand or set on music stands.

• Readers look straight out toward the audience or at an angle, rather than at each other.

A very different style, designed for greater appeal to young audiences, has been developed by Chamber Readers, the group that provided my own start in reader's theater. Chamber Readers is a professional, nonprofit reader's theater company in Humboldt County, California, promoting reading and literature since 1975. For most of its first two decades—including my years with the group—it was directed by Jean Wagner, a founding member. Considered a local institution, Chamber Readers has performed yearly in almost every public school in the county.

Like traditional reader's theater, the Chamber Readers style is based on the visible use of scripts and the suggestive power of language—but it adds a good deal of movement as well. Though that takes more effort, it's also more rewarding and involving for both readers and audience.

Briefly, the distinctive features of the Chamber Readers style are:

• Characters portray the action described in the story. Where possible, the portrayal is literal, with characters moving around the stage much as in a play. Where necessary, it's suggestive, as with simple mime devices like walking in place.

• Though narrators look mostly at the audience, characters look mostly at each other.

• Scripts in sturdy binders are held in one hand, leaving the other hand free for acting.

• A set of low stools and perhaps one or more high stools serve as versatile stage scenery or props.

The following tips on staging are based on the Chamber Readers style. But remember, these are suggestions only. I hope you'll feel free to use or develop whatever style will be most enjoyable to you and your readers.

By the way, *stage* here refers simply to your performance area—which could be the front of a classroom, or an open space in a one-room library, or one end of a school gym or cafeteria. An actual stage isn't needed.

Equipment

For reader's theater, you really need nothing but scripts. Still, a little basic equipment can add a lot. Here are some recommended items:

- **Script binders.** Sturdy ring binders are best. Whatever you use, make sure the pages turn easily. Onstage the binder may also become a prop, standing in for a book, a notepad, the surface of a table.
- **Smocks.** These give the readers a team look, yet are also neutral—so readers can easily change roles in the minds of the audience. The smock can be a simple rectangle of cloth with a head hole, fastened together at the sides.
- **Low stools.** Stools of chair height are your most useful props. For some stories, you won't need any; for others, you may need one for each reader. *They must be solid enough to stand on!*
- **High stools.** One or two should be enough. These too should be solid enough to stand on—if you'll allow such risk in the pursuit of art.
- **Folding screens.** I refer to those freestanding, portable room dividers made of two or more panels hinged together. Though not required or even often seen in reader's theater, they're fun to use if available, providing alternative ways to handle entrances, exits, and some special effects.
- **Small props.** These can sometimes add nice touches—as when a Pied Piper has a tin whistle to play.

Script Handling

The trick with scripts is to handle them so they can be referred to easily but don't seriously restrict movement or distract the audience. The script is held by one hand alone, leaving the other hand free for acting. For a relaxed grip, readers simply let the binder spine rest in the palm. But if readers are moving a lot and need a firmer hold, they can reach forward and grip the binder's top edge, while the binder rests on the upturned forearm.

Right-handers hold a script with their left hand, left-handers with their right. But sometimes a reader might have to switch hands, if a particular hand is needed for stage action, or if looking at the script turns the reader's face too far from the audience. At times, a reader might even have to put the script down!

Though readers don't need to memorize, they should know their parts well enough to look up from their scripts about half the time. (I call this "half-memorizing.") When they *do* look down, it's only with the eyes, keeping the head straight up. In general, it's best to look down when *starting* a sentence rather than when ending it, since the end is where delivery should be strongest.

You will have to be flexible in how scripts are used. A character who has to look steeply upward for much of a scene may have to memorize part of the script. A narrator who has a long speech may have to run a finger down the page to keep the place. A reader who won't have a hand free to turn a page when needed can instead place that page backward in the binder to get two pages facing.

The Set

In theater lingo, the *set* is all the constructed "scenery" and large props placed onstage to represent one or more locations. In reader's theater, you don't *build* sets, but you can *suggest* them. What the narrator describes is made real by the characters' movements and mime. If a reader opens a door, we see it. If readers hang ornaments on a Christmas tree, we know right where it is.

Stools are among your chief aids for suggesting sets, as well as being practical props. Three low stools in a semicircle can be a dining room. Two low stools close by each other can be a bench in a park, or a roof ridge atop a house. A single high stool can be a throne room. A high stool with a low stool next to it can be a tree to climb, or a mountain. An area with no stools can be anything at all!

As in regular theater, you start designing your set by figuring out what locations your script calls for. Then you position those locations on your stage in whatever arrangement works and looks best. Aim for ease of reader movement, stage balance, and openness to the audience.

Readers can move to different parts of the stage for different scenes. Or they can stay where they are and "change the set," perhaps by moving the stools quickly to new positions. Or the set can move to them! For instance, a reader could move from room to room in a house just by walking in place, climbing some stairs, and opening some doors—all without moving an inch.

Reader Movement

After designing your set, decide where your readers will start and where they will go. As in regular theater, characters should be placed to help them face the audience as much as possible when speaking. And don't forget the narrators! They can be placed wherever you want, but they usually stand forward at either end of the stage.

Characters normally stay "offstage" until needed in a scene. But in reader's theater, this simply means that they stay turned with "back to audience"—*BTA*, for short. That indicates to the audience that the readers are out of the picture, even if visible. While staying BTA, the readers might either be sitting on stools or standing somewhere out of the other readers' way, usually at the back of the stage. When it's time to "enter," they simply "turn in" and perhaps move forward. To "exit," they do the opposite: "turn out" and perhaps move to the back. Narrators always face in, though, even when not reading for a long while.

In regular theater, the curtain or the lights coming down indicates a "scene change"—a jump in time or place. In reader's theater, this change is shown instead by some kind of break in movement. For instance, the characters can all "freeze" in place like statues. Or they can turn BTA, freeze, then come back in. Or they can freeze, then cross the stage for the next scene. But you can do without any break at all if one scene flows smoothly into the next without a jump.

Drawing a series of movement diagrams can help you spot problems, save time during rehearsal, and jog your memory the next time you use the script. In one simple diagram system, circles are low stools, double circles are high stools, crosses are readers, and arrows show movement. The diagrams are oriented to audience view, with the stage edge at bottom. (See Figure 2, next page.)

Mime and Sound Effects

Whatever action is described in the script, readers should try either to do it or else to suggest it through mime. If someone is eating, we should see the fork carried to the mouth. If someone is hanging in the air, we should see the arm pulled tight by the floating balloon. If someone is racing a horse, we should see the galloping hooves.

The key word here is "suggest," because the movements are often far from realistic. For instance, it's hard to take off a coat realistically when one hand holds a script. Readers quickly learn to sleep sitting up, with their heads bent to the side. And walking in place is a reader's favorite mode of travel.

Though formal mime techniques aren't required, they do add polish to a performance. It's always good to draw on proven tricks for walking in place, climbing up or down stairs or ropes or ladders, lifting or pulling heavy objects, flying, falling, and so on. Look for a beginning book on mime, or invite a local mime to conduct a workshop.

Part of successful group mime is being aware of the invisible. If a stool is meant to be a chair at a table, make sure no one walks through the table! Even a door that's invisible shouldn't shift position as different people pass through it. If two characters look at a picture on the wall, they will hopefully agree where it is!

Sounds in the story too should be added where possible—explosions, wind, bees, roosters, whatever. To help the illusion, this is usually done by readers with backs to the audience.

Figure 2. Sample Movement Diagrams

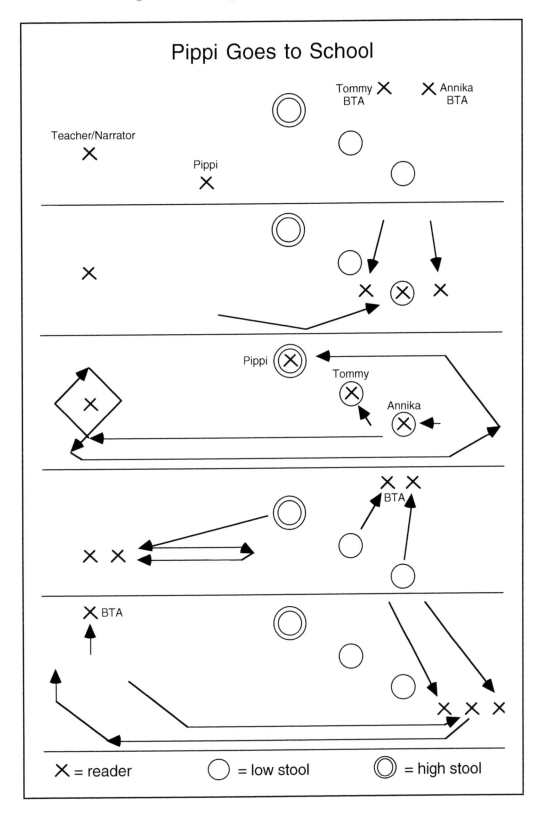

Focus

Focus refers to where a reader is looking. Most of the time, it's simple: Narrators use *audience focus*—they look straight at the audience, even when the audience isn't looking at *them*. Characters use *onstage focus*—they look at whoever they're talking to, just as in plays or real life.

But sometimes you might want characters to use *offstage focus*. (See Figure 3, below.) The readers imagine a screen facing them, as wide as the stage, set up at the front edge of the audience. On this screen they imagine projected images of all the readers. Then instead of talking straight to each other, they talk to each other's projection on the screen. If you prefer, you can "move" the screen farther from the readers, as long as everyone agrees where it is.

Figure 3. Offstage Focus

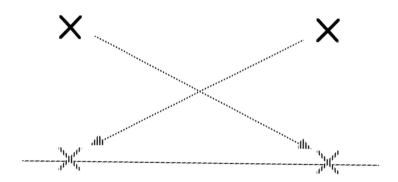

The most important use of offstage focus is to help create illusions of distance or height. With offstage focus, two characters on the same stage can shout and wave at each other as if a mile apart. Or if one looks upward and one looks downward, you have a midget talking to a giant, or a woman in a window talking to a man in the street.

Audience focus too can at times be used by characters, for making comments directly to the audience. It might also be used to draw the audience into the story—for example, if the audience suddenly becomes a hill completely covered with cats.

At times, a narrator too can use onstage or offstage focus. This is good for interactions between narrators or between narrator and character—which can be fun or startling because they defy the convention of narrator isolation. It could also be used to insert the narrator partway into the story as a personal observer and commenter. (Think of the Stage Manager in Thornton Wilder's *Our Town*, a play sharing many conventions with this style of reader's theater.)

Finally, a reader who doubles as narrator and character might use a different focus for each, with a shift in focus signaling a shift in roles.

Beginnings and Endings

The effectiveness of your performance as a whole and of each story within it is enhanced when all are "set off" with proper beginning and endings. The following are recommended:

At the beginning of the performance come a few words of greeting and introduction from one or more readers, who identify the group and tell anything else about why it's there and what it's presenting.

Then before each story is performed, it's introduced individually, again by one or more readers, who tell something about the story or the author or the performance. The intro can present a fact or an idea or an anecdote or even a question. Just don't give away the plot!

Intros should always be prepared ahead of time, whether or not they're written down. They're most effective when delivered informally but can also be memorized, delivered from notes, or just read directly. Generally, no more than a few sentences is needed or wanted. Often the content is left to the reader and can vary according to who gives that intro during a particular performance.

Following the story intro, the title and the author are announced, along with the name of the larger work if your script is an excerpt. Most often, the announcement is tacked onto the intro by a simple, "And now, here is . . . ," or something similar. Then the readers wait to begin till they're all in place and frozen and the audience is quiet and attentive.

As the story ends, the last words are spoken slowly and with exaggerated rhythm, so the audience knows the story is over. Everyone recognizes the ending "*hap*-pily *ev*-er *af*-ter." But the same effect can be achieved with almost any words by reading them in a "slow three," using stressed syllables to form three strong "beats."

Next, the readers freeze for a long moment to break the action. Then they close their scripts, face the audience squarely, and bow all together. To help time this sequence, you can have the readers count slowly to themselves. You might also pick one reader toward the front of the stage—probably a narrator—to lead it.

For individual stories, *nothing* follows the bow. Any comments added at the end can only weaken the story's impact. But the final story is followed by a few words of thanks and farewell.

When rehearsing, always include your beginnings and endings along with the rest, to make sure they'll go smoothly in performance.

Once young people have a general idea of how reader's theater works, they can take over much of the staging themselves. In fact, they often beat adults at developing mime.

After all, pretending is part of their profession.

Tips on Reading

Mumble, mumble,
Stop and stumble.
Pages turn
and readers fumble.

If this sounds like a description of your reader's theater efforts, try giving your readers the following tips.

Preparing

First, here are instructions your readers can follow—individually or in a group—to prepare their scripts and get familiar with their parts.

• Highlight your speeches in your copy of the script. Mark only words you will *speak*—not the identifying role tags or the stage directions. (Yellow non-fluorescent marker works best.)

• Underline the words that tell about anything you'll need to act out—words in either the stage directions or *other* readers' speeches. If you're given extra stage directions later, write them in the margin in *pencil*.

• Read through your part silently. If there are words you don't understand or aren't sure how to pronounce, look them up in a dictionary. If there are words you must remember to stress, underline them. If there are places you'll need to pause between sentences, mark them with a couple of slashes (//). For instance, a narrator must sometimes pause to help the audience know there's a change of scene or time.

• Read through your part out loud. If you're a character, think about how that character would sound. Should you try a funny voice? How would the character feel about what's happening in the story? Can you speak as if you were feeling that?

• Stand up and read through the script again. If you're a character, try out faces and movements. Would your character stand or move in a special way? Can you do that? If possible, try all this in front of a mirror.

Even before you give your readers their scripts, you can help them by reading them the script or its source story. Effective modeling will give them a head start against any difficulties. You might also want to discuss the difference between characters and narrators. ("In the story, character parts are *inside* the quotation marks, and narrator parts are *outside*.")

Rehearsing

Here are pointers your readers should remember both in rehearsal and performance.

• Hold your script at a steady height, but make sure it doesn't hide your face. If there's anyone you can't see in the front row of the audience, your script is too high.

• While you speak, try to look up often, not just at your script. When you do look down at it, keep your head up and move just your eyes.

• S-l-o-w d-o-w-n. Say each syl-la-ble clear-ly.

• TALK LOUD! You have to be heard by the little old deaf lady in the back row.

• *Speak with feeling.* Audiences love a ham!

• Stand and sit straight. Keep your hands and feet still, if they're not doing anything useful!

• Face the audience as much as you can, whether you're moving or standing still. If you're rehearsing without an audience, pretend it's there anyway and remember where it is.

• Narrators, you're important even when the audience isn't looking at you. You control the story! Be sure to give the characters enough time to do what they must. And remember that you're talking to the audience, not yourself.

• Characters, you give the story its life! Remember to *be* your character even when you're not speaking, and be sure to react to the other characters.

To help your readers get full vocal power, have them check their breathing. To do this, they should place their hands on their stomachs and inhale. If they're really filling their lungs, their hands will be pushed *out*. (The diaphragm muscle gives the lungs more room by pushing down on the stomach, making it expand forward.) If their hands move *in,* it means they're filling only the top parts of their lungs.

Tongue twisters and other vocal exercises can help your readers speak more clearly. You might even warm them up with such exercises before your rehearsals and performances.

To help your readers hold themselves straight, ask them to imagine a string tied to their chest, pulling up.

Performing

Before an actual performance, discuss with your readers the "what-ifs."

- If the audience laughs, stop speaking till they can hear you again.
- If someone talks in the audience, don't pay attention.
- If someone walks into the room, don't look.
- If you make a mistake, pretend it was right.
- If you drop something, try to leave it at least till the audience is looking somewhere else.
- If a reader forgets to read, see if you can read their part instead, or make something up, or maybe just skip over it. But *don't* whisper or signal to the reader!
- If a reader falls on their rear end, pretend they didn't.

Finally, a couple of reminders for the director: Have fun, and tell your readers what they're doing well!

Part 3 ~ An RT Workshop

In this section, you'll find everything else you need to start with reader's theater in the classroom or library, or to conduct your own reader's theater workshop for adults. The materials come from my own workshops for teachers and librarians, and were designed so they could be carried into the classroom or library the next day—as they often have been for ages down to 9 or 10. All the materials may be freely copied, shared, or performed for any noncommercial purpose, except they may not be posted online without permission.

The materials include:

- A sample list of materials to have on hand.
- Sample outlines for workshops of various lengths.
- Instructor notes and handouts I use in the sessions themselves.
- A set of 25 worksheets for small-group exercises in team scripting, staging, and dramatic reading.

The worksheets supplied are enough for a session with 100 adults, or for four rounds with 25 young people. All are excerpts from my own picture books and stories. For other exercise material, I recommend Arnold Lobel's *Fables*, featuring complete stories on single pages and suited to a wide range of ages. The benefit of doing the exercises with complete stories is that you wind up with pieces actually ready to perform for outside audiences.

Like Part 2 of this book, my workshops come in three modules covering scripting, staging, and dramatic reading. Typically, each module runs from 1 to 1½ hours. Though each one builds on the one previous, the scripting module can stand alone—which is how I usually offer it. Here are its basic parts:

Introduction and overview. A brief look at what's to come.

Sample script reading. This is a warm-up reading with volunteers. It wakes everyone up, provides a first taste of reader's theater, gives you a specific example to refer to, and lets your readers know they're in for some fun.

The scripts in Part 1 of this book were selected especially for this activity. Choose your script to include the greatest number of readers available. "The Legend of Lightning Larry" will take the most readers, "Peddler Polly and the Story Stealer" a smaller number, and "The Baker's Dozen" the smallest.

Each script copy you hand out should have speeches for a single role already highlighted. I like to assign roles randomly by handing out scripts "first come, first served," though making sure that female roles go to females. Be sure to have an extra script copy for yourself, in case your readers need prompting. For reader placement, it's enough at this point to just stand them at the front of your space, though you might want to at least place the narrators at the ends.

Talk on scripting. I work from the instructor notes supplied here, filling in with additional comments and with references to the script just read. The notes are basically a summary of the corresponding chapter in Part 2 of this book, so for best results, first study that chapter yourself.

Team scripting exercise. This is the core of the module. I let the readers divide themselves into groups of four, with any leftover readers added to groups as fifth members. No group may have more than five, or fewer than four; and if possible, at least two in each group should be female.

Each group is then assigned one of the worksheets, with a copy of it given to each reader. (To handle groups with an extra member, be sure to have five copies ready for each worksheet.) Finally, everyone listens to these directions, as found also in the notes:

1. Read through the story silently.
2. As a group, identify the roles in the story and divide them among you.
3. Go over the story together, deciding who will read what and also what to cut. On your own sheet, in pencil, cross out the cuts and underline your own speeches. (You don't need to mark the speeches of others—but if you want to anyway, then put a circled name, initial, or number above where each reader will start.)
4. Try out your script by reading together. Go back and change it as needed.

In fifteen or twenty minutes, each group should have a script! Young people as well as adults are capable of team scripting. In fact, the only time I've seen kids have trouble is when an adult tried to "help" them.

The value of team scripting goes beyond its use as an exercise, because the same method can be applied later to creating longer scripts for performance. That's right: If you don't want to script, your readers can do it for you! For a more finished product, though, you or they might compile the results into a "master script" in standard format.

Small group performances. Each group performs its script for the others. In this first reading, staging and dramatics are not concerns, but if a group wants to ham a little, that's fine. I usually comment briefly on each script, pointing out interesting choices as well as things that worked especially well.

There's no sense in being critical here—the exercise is mostly for inspiration and encouragement.

Of course, if there might not be enough time for all groups to perform, you'll want to warn of that beforehand.

Added modules on staging and dramatic reading follow the same basic pattern. Each includes a brief talk—from notes that summarize a chapter in Part 2—plus continued work in small groups with the pieces scripted earlier, and finally, performance with comments. In addition, the staging module begins with a staging of the sample script that was read at the beginning, to show how it can be done. If time is short, you can omit the small group performances from the scripting and staging modules, saving that part for the last.

For adults, I add a talk about key reader's theater resources, focusing of course on my own Web site and books. A list of those and additional resources is on the final handout supplied here.

And for any age group, if I have time at the end, I get everyone on their feet and teach basic mime techniques to use in staging. That's always a fun way to finish.

Though the materials presented here are my own, my scripting module derives from a workshop developed by earlier members of Chamber Readers, the professional reader's theater company I worked with, and especially by Chamber Reader James Floss, my own instructor in reader's theater at Humboldt State University. Thanks to James and Chamber Readers!

Sample Materials List

RT Workshop—Materials List

Outline

Instructor notes

Handouts

Scripting worksheets (5 copies each)

Sample scripts (assigned and highlighted)

RT books for display

Sample Outlines

Reader's Theater: From Story to Script

1 hour

5	Intro and Overview
10	Activity—Read Sample Script
10	Talk—"From Story to Script"
15	Small Group Exercise—Script and Rehearse
15	Presentation—Small Group Performances
5	Talk—"RT Resources"

_____

60 minutes

Reader's Theater: From Story to Script

$1^1/_2$ hours

5	Intro and Overview
10	Activity—Read Sample Script
10	Talk—"From Story to Script"
20	Small Group Exercise—Script and Rehearse
30	Presentation—Small Group Performances
5	Talk—"RT Resources"
5	Q&A
5	Activity—Mime Lesson (Optional)

———

90 minutes

Reader's Theater: For the Love of Reading

$3\frac{1}{2}$ hours

5	Intro and Overview
10	Activity—Read Sample Script
10	Talk—"From Story to Script"
15	Small Group Exercise—Script and Rehearse
20	Presentation—Small Group Performances
15	BREAK
30	Activity—Stage Sample Script
10	Talk—"From Script to Stage"
15	Small Group Exercise—Stage and Rehearse
20	Presentation—Small Group Performances
15	BREAK
10	Talk—"Tips for Readers"
10	Small Group Exercise—Rehearse
10	Presentation—Small Group Performances
5	Talk—"RT Resources"
5	Q&A
5	Activity—Mime Lesson (Optional)

210 minutes

Notes and Handouts

Reader's Theater—From Story to Script

1. Almost any story can be performed, but some are easier and work better than others. In general, look for stories that are simple and lively, with lots of dialog or action and with not too many scenes or characters.

2. Start by seeing what speaking parts or *roles* are in the story. There are two kinds: *Narrators* tell the story. *Characters* are *in* the story. Another way to say it: Character parts are in quotation marks, narrator parts are outside.

3. Match the roles to your readers.

—If you have too many readers:
   • You can have two or more narrators.
   • Some characters too can be split into two parts.
   • Or you can have people who act but don't say anything.

—If you don't have enough readers:
   • Some readers can be more than one character—but not at once!
   • Or you can take out characters, or combine two into one.
   • Or the characters can be narrators too.

4. Feel free to take out parts of the text to make your script livelier, simpler to understand, or just easier to perform. But make sure the story still makes sense! Here are some things you might want to "cut":
   • "He said" and "she said" lines (called *tag lines*).
   • Long descriptions.
   • Characters or scenes that are less important.

5. Other kinds of changes you might make:
   • Add speeches for characters who have few or no lines.
   • Convert narrator comments to stage directions.
   • Simplify language by replacing difficult words and splitting sentences.
   • Replace language that is sexist or demeaning.
   • Add reading aids—word stresses, commas, interpretive stage directions.

6. Format the script so it's easy to read, with big margins and some space between the lines. Readers can highlight their own speeches and write extra stage directions in the margins in pencil.

Team Scripting Exercise

1. Read through the story silently.
2. As a group, identify the roles in the story and divide them among you.
3. Go over the story together, deciding who will read what and also what to cut. On your own sheet, in pencil, cross out the cuts and underline your own speeches. (You don't need to mark the speeches of others—but if you want to anyway, then put a circled name, initial, or number above where each reader will start.)
4. Try out your script by reading together. Go back and change it as needed.

Reader's Theater—Sample Script Page

NARRATOR 1: Within a year, a daughter came to the king and his favorite wife. He named her Savitri, after the goddess.

NARRATOR 2: Beauty and intelligence were the princess Savitri's, and eyes that shone like the sun. So splendid was she, people thought she herself was a goddess.

NARRATOR 3: Yet when the time came for her to marry, no man asked for her. Her father told her,

KING 1: Weak men turn away from radiance like yours. Go out and find a man worthy of you. Then I will arrange the marriage.

NARRATOR 1: In the company of servants and councilors, Savitri traveled from place to place.

NARRATOR 2: After many days, she came upon a hermitage by a river crossing. Here lived many who had left the towns and cities for a life of prayer and study.

NARRATOR 3: Savitri entered the hall of worship and bowed to the eldest teacher. As they spoke, a young man with shining eyes came into the hall. He guided another man, old and blind.

SAVITRI: *(softly, to the teacher)* Who is that young man?

TEACHER: *(smiling)* That is Prince Satyavan. He guides his father, a king whose realm was conquered. It is well that Satyavan's name means "Son of Truth," for no man is richer in virtue.

NARRATOR 1: When Savitri returned home, she found her father with the holy seer called Narada.

KING 1: Daughter, have you found a man you wish to marry?

SAVITRI: Yes, father. His name is Satyavan.

Reader's Theater—From Script to Stage

There are many styles of reader's theater. This one takes a little more effort than some others, but it's also more rewarding for both readers and audience.

1. All you really need is scripts, but other good items to have are script binders, smocks, low and high stools, and the occasional small prop.

2. Readers should hold their scripts with one hand, leaving the other hand free for acting. They should try to look up about half the time. When they look down at their scripts, they should keep their heads up and move only their eyes.

3. Start planning your staging by identifying the locations your script calls for. Then decide where you'll place them onstage. Aim for ease of reader movement, stage balance, and openness to the audience. Stools can help "suggest" locations and can be moved for scene changes.

4. Next, plan reader position and movement. Place your characters so they'll face the audience as much as possible when reading. Don't forget your narrators—they normally stand forward at either end. Drawing a series of diagrams will help.

5. When not in a scene, characters "exit" or go "offstage" by turning their "back to audience"*(BTA)* and sometimes also moving to the back. (Narrators, though, always stay facing forward.) A "scene change"—a jump in time or place—can be signaled by a "freeze," often with all characters first turning BTA.

6. Characters act out or mime the actions described in the script. Useful mime devices include walking in place and sleeping upright.

7. Sound effects can be added by readers turned BTA.

8. Readers need to be clear about their *focus*—where they will look.

> • *Audience focus* means looking straight at the audience. This is standard for narrators.

> • *Onstage focus* means looking directly at who you're talking to. This is standard for characters.

> • *Offstage focus* means looking at who you're talking to, but in an imaginary projection toward the audience. This can be used by characters to help create illusions of distance or height.

9. **Beginnings:** The story title and author are announced, possibly after a brief introduction. (Don't give away the plot!) The story begins once all the readers are in place and frozen and the audience is quiet.

10. **Endings:** The last words of the story are read slowly and with enhanced rhythm, so the audience knows the story is over. Then the readers freeze for a moment, then close their scripts, face the audience, and bow together.

Reader's Theater—Tips for Readers

1. Hold your script at a steady height. Don't let it hide your face!

2. Try to look up often. When you look down at your script, keep your head up and move just your eyes.

3. S-l-o-w d-o-w-n. Say each syl-la-ble clear-ly. (To help with that, try practicing tongue twisters.)

4. TALK LOUD! Make sure the last row of the audience can easily hear you. For good vocal power, make sure you breathe fully. (When you inhale, your stomach should push *out*.)

5. *Speak with feeling.* Audiences love a ham!

6. Stand and sit straight. (Imagine a string tied to your chest, pulling up.) Keep your hands and feet still, if they're doing nothing useful!

7. Face the audience—or wherever the audience would be—as much as you can.

8. Narrators are important! You control the story! Make sure you give the characters enough time to do what they must. If a sudden scene change falls in the middle of your speech, pause a moment to signal the break. And remember, you're talking to the audience, not to yourself.

9. Characters give the story its life. Try to sound, look, and move like you think your character would. Ask yourself, "What is this character feeling?"—then act like that! (It's good to practice all this in front of a mirror.) Remember to *be* your character even when you're not speaking, and be sure to react to other characters.

10. Above all, have fun!

Reader's Theater—RT Resources

Books and Articles

Readers on Stage: Resources for Reader's Theater, With Tips, Play Scripts, and Worksheets, Aaron Shepard, Shepard Publications, 2004.

Stories on Stage: Scripts for Reader's Theater, Aaron Shepard, H. W. Wilson, 1993; Shepard Publications, 2005.

Folktales on Stage: 16 Scripts for Reader's Theater From Folk and Fairy Tales of the World, Aaron Shepard, Shepard Publications, 2004.

Presenting Reader's Theater: Plays and Poems to Read Aloud, Caroline Feller Bauer, H. W. Wilson, 1987.

From the Page to the Stage: The Educator's Complete Guide to Readers Theatre, Shirlee Sloyer, Teacher Ideas Press, 2003.

Institute Book of Readers Theatre: A Practical Guide for School, Theater, & Community, William Adams, Institute for Readers Theatre, 2003.

Readers Theatre for Beginning Readers, Suzanne I. Barchers, Teacher Ideas Press, 1993.

Frantic Frogs and Other Frankly Fractured Folktales for Readers Theatre, Anthony D. Fredericks, Teacher Ideas Press, 1993.

Online—Web Sites

Aaron Shepard's RT Page, www.aaronshep.com/rt.

Readers Theatre Digest, www.readerstheatredigest.com.

Teaching Heart ~ Reader's Theater Scripts and Plays, www.teachingheart.net/readerstheater.htm.

Literacy Connections ~ Readers' Theater, www.literacyconnections.com/ReadersTheater.html.

Online—Email List

ReadersTheater, groups.yahoo.com/group/ReadersTheater.

Suppliers

Readers Theatre Script Service, www.readerstheatreinstitute.com.
Scripts for Schools, www.scriptsforschools.com.
Storycart Press, www.storycart.com.
Playbooks, www.eplaybooks.com.

Scripting Worksheets

Master Man • By Aaron Shepard

When Shettu got home, she told Shadusa what had happened.

"Master Man?" yelled Shadusa. "He can't call himself that! *I'm* Master Man. I'll have to teach that fellow a lesson."

"Oh, husband, don't!" pleaded Shettu. "If the baby is so strong, think what the father must be like. You'll get yourself killed."

But Shadusa said, "We'll see about that!"

The next morning, Shadusa set out early and walked till he came to the well. He threw in the bucket—*splash*—then he pulled on the rope. But though he tugged and he heaved, he could not lift the bucket.

Just then the woman with the baby walked up.

"Wait a minute," said Shadusa. "What do you think you're doing?"

"I'm getting water, of course," answered the woman.

"Well, you can't," said Shadusa. "The bucket won't come up."

The woman set down the baby, who quickly pulled up the bucket and filled his mother's calabash.

"Wah!" yelled Shadusa. "How did he do that?"

"It's easy," said the woman, "when your father is Master Man."

Shadusa gulped and thought about going home. But instead he thrust out his chest and said, "I want to meet this fellow, so I can show him who's the *real* Master Man."

"Oh, I wouldn't do that," said the woman. "He devours men like you! But suit yourself."

So Shadusa followed the woman back to her compound. Inside the fenced yard was a gigantic fireplace, and beside it was a pile of huge bones.

"What's all this?" asked Shadusa.

"Well, you see," said the woman, "our hut is so small that my husband must come out here to eat his elephants."

Just then they heard a great ROAR, so loud that Shadusa had to cover his ears. Then the ground began to shake, until Shadusa could hardly stand.

"What's that?" he shouted.

"That's Master Man."

"Oh, no!" wailed Shadusa. "You weren't fooling. I've got to get out of here!"

The Sea King's Daughter • By Aaron Shepard

Taken from the picture book *The Sea King's Daughter: A Russian Legend,* told by Aaron Shepard, illustrated by Gennady Spirin, Atheneum, 1997. Copyright © 1997, 2004 Aaron Shepard. May be copied for any noncommercial purpose. *Novgorod* is pronounced "NOV-go-rod." *Sadko* is pronounced "SOD-ko." *Volkhov* is pronounced "VOLE-kove." *Gusli* is pronounced "GOOSE-lee." *Volkhova* is pronounced "VOLE-ko-vah." More at **www.aaronshep.com**.

"Is there another such city as Novgorod in all the world?" Sadko would say. "Is there any better place to be?" Yet sometimes Sadko was lonely too. The maidens who danced gaily to his music would often smile at him—but they were rich and he was poor, and not one of them would think of being his.

One lonely evening, Sadko walked sadly beyond the city walls and down along the broad River Volkhov. He came to his favorite spot on the bank and set his twelve-string *gusli* on his lap. Gentle waves brushed the shore, and moonlight shimmered on the water.

"My lovely River Volkhov," he said with a sigh. "Rich man, poor man—it's all the same to you. If only you were a woman! I'd marry you and live with you here in the city I love."

Sadko plucked a sad tune, then a peaceful one, then a merry one. The tinkling notes of his gusli floated over the Volkhov.

All at once the river grew rough, and strong waves began to slap the bank. "Heaven help me!" cried Sadko as a large shape rose from the water. Before him stood a huge man, with a pearl-encrusted crown atop a flowing mane of seaweed.

"Musician," said the man, "behold the King of the Sea. To this river I have come to visit one of my daughters, the Princess Volkhova. Your sweet music reached us on the river bottom, where it pleased us greatly."

"Thank you, Your Majesty," stammered Sadko.

"Soon I will return to my own palace," said the King. "I wish you to play there at a feast."

"Gladly," said Sadko. "But where is it? And how do I get there?"

"Why, under the sea, of course! I'm sure you'll find your way. But meanwhile, you need not wait for your reward."

Something large jumped from the river and flopped at Sadko's feet. A fish with golden scales! As Sadko watched in amazement, it stiffened and turned to solid gold.

"Your Majesty, you are too generous!"

"Say no more about it!" said the King. "Music is worth far more than gold. If the world were fair, you'd have your fill of riches!" And with a splash, he sank in the river and was gone.

#3

King o' the Cats • By Aaron Shepard

Taken from the picture book *King o' the Cats*, told by Aaron Shepard, illustrated by Kristin Sorra, Atheneum, 2004. Copyright © 1995, 1997, 2004 Aaron Shepard. May be copied for any noncommercial purpose. More at **www.aaronshep.com**.

"What in the world . . . ?" muttered Peter. "There shouldn't be anyone there, this time of night. And how'd they get in, anyway?"

Peter pulled on a coat, crossed the yard, and quietly unlocked the back door. As he crept through the vestry, he heard a sound from the church. *Meow, meow . . . .*

"Sounds like a cat," murmured Peter. "But I never knew a cat to light a candle."

He peered around the curtain hung at the church entrance, and what he saw made him gasp. There was not *one* cat, but *hundreds* of cats, of every size and coloring. They filled the pews, and all of them sat upright just like people.

On the steps to the altar, a big black cat—the biggest cat Peter had ever seen—was kneeling with his head bowed. Standing above him with paws upraised was a black cat in bishop's robes, intoning, *"Meow, meow . . . ."*

An altar kitten approached with a velvet pillow on which lay a small golden crown. The bishop lifted the crown and solemnly placed it on the kneeling cat's head.

The church exploded with cries of *Meow, meow!* Peter didn't wait to see more. He raced through the vestry and back to his cottage, where he jumped into bed and stayed trembling under the covers till morning.

Bright and early, Peter was over to see Father Allen. The priest was reading in the conservatory, his black cat Tom curled up on his lap.

"Good morning, Peter," said the priest. "What brings you here so early?"

"Father Allen, I came to tell you about something terribly weird in the church last night. I saw these lights and I went over to check, and I heard a *meow*—"

"Meow," said the priest's cat, Tom.

"Yes, just like that," said Peter. "And when I looked, there were hundreds of cats in the church. And there was this one big black cat, and he was kneeling in front, and their bishop was crowning him—"

Father Allen was looking at him sternly. "Peter, do you remember what I told you about wild stories?"

"Of course I do, Father."

"Then let's have no more of this, all right?"

The Princess Mouse • By Aaron Shepard

Mikko walked through the forest for hours without seeing a soul. But at last he came to a cottage deep in the woods.

"I knew I'd find a sweetheart!" said Mikko. But when he went inside, he saw no one.

"All this way for nothing," he said sadly.

"Maybe not!" came a tiny voice.

Mikko looked around, but the only living thing in sight was a little mouse on a table. Standing on its hind legs, it gazed at him with large, bright eyes.

"Did you say something?" he asked it.

"Of course I did! Now, why don't you tell me your name and what you came for?"

Mikko had never talked with a mouse, but he felt it only polite to reply. "My name is Mikko, and I've come looking for a sweetheart."

The mouse squealed in delight. "Why, Mikko, I'll gladly be your sweetheart!"

"But you're only a mouse," said Mikko.

"That may be true," she said, "but I can still love you faithfully. Besides, even a mouse can be special! Come feel my fur."

With one finger, Mikko stroked the mouse's back. "Why, it feels like velvet! Just like the gown of a princess!"

"That's right, Mikko." And as he petted her, she sang to him prettily.

> "Mikko's sweetheart will I be.
> What a fine young man is he!
> Gown of velvet I do wear,
> Like a princess fine and rare."

Mikko looked into those large, bright eyes and thought she really was quite nice, for a mouse. And since he'd found no one else anyway, he said, "All right, little mouse, you can be my sweetheart."

"Oh, Mikko!" she said happily. "I promise you won't be sorry."

Mikko wasn't so sure, but he just stroked her fur and smiled.

The Baker's Dozen • By Aaron Shepard

Taken from the picture book *The Baker's Dozen: A Saint Nicholas Tale,* told by Aaron Shepard, illustrated by Wendy Edelson, Atheneum, 1995. Copyright © 1995, 1997, 2004 Aaron Shepard. May be copied for any noncommercial purpose. More at **www.aaronshep.com**.

In the Dutch colonial town later known as Albany, New York, there lived a baker, Van Amsterdam, who was as honest as he could be. Each morning, he checked and balanced his scales, and he took great care to give his customers exactly what they paid for—not more and not less.

Van Amsterdam's shop was always busy, because people trusted him, and because he was a good baker as well. And never was the shop busier than in the days before December 6, when the Dutch celebrate Saint Nicholas Day.

At that time of year, people flocked to the baker's shop to buy his fine Saint Nicholas cookies. Made of gingerbread, iced in red and white, they looked just like Saint Nicholas as the Dutch know him—tall and thin, with a high, red bishop's cap, and a long, red bishop's cloak.

One Saint Nicholas Day morning, the baker was just ready for business, when the door of his shop flew open. In walked an old woman, wrapped in a long black shawl.

"I have come for a dozen of your Saint Nicholas cookies."

Taking a tray, Van Amsterdam counted out twelve cookies. He started to wrap them, but the woman reached out and stopped him.

"I asked for a dozen. You have given me only twelve."

"Madam," said the baker, "everyone knows that a dozen *is* twelve."

"But I say a dozen is thirteen," said the woman. "Give me one more."

Van Amsterdam was not a man to bear foolishness. "Madam, my customers get exactly what they pay for—not more and not less."

"Then you may keep the cookies," the woman said. She turned to go, but stopped at the door.

"Van Amsterdam! However honest you may be, your heart is small and your fist is tight. *Fall again, mount again, learn how to count again!*"

Then she was gone.

From that day, everything went wrong in Van Amsterdam's bakery. His bread rose too high or not at all. His pies were sour or too sweet. His cakes crumbled or were chewy. His cookies were burnt or doughy. Before long, most of his customers were going to other bakers.

"That old woman has bewitched me," said the baker to himself. "Is this how my honesty is rewarded?"

Savitri: A Tale of Ancient India • By Aaron Shepard

Finally, only three days remained. Savitri entered the hall of worship and faced the sacred fire. There she prayed for three days and nights, not eating or sleeping.

The sun was just rising when Savitri at last left the hall. She saw Satyavan heading for the forest, an ax on his shoulder.

Savitri rushed to his side. "I will come with you."

"Stay here, my love," said Satyavan. "You should eat and rest."

But Savitri said, "My heart is set on going."

Hand in hand, Savitri and Satyavan walked over wooded hills. They smelled the blossoms on flowering trees and paused beside clear streams. The cries of peacocks echoed through the woods.

While Savitri rested, Satyavan chopped firewood from a fallen tree. Suddenly, he dropped his ax.

"My head aches," he said.

Savitri rushed to him. She laid him down in the shade of a tree, his head on her lap.

"My body is burning!" said Satyavan. "What is wrong with me?"

Satyavan's eyes closed. His breathing slowed.

Savitri looked up. Coming through the woods to meet them was a princely man. He shone, though his skin was darker than the darkest night. His eyes and his robe were the red of blood.

Trembling, Savitri asked, "Who are you?"

A deep, gentle voice replied. "Princess, you see me only by the power of your prayer and fasting. I am Yama, god of death. Now is the time I must take the spirit of Satyavan."

Yama took a small noose and passed it through Satyavan's breast, as if through air. He drew out a tiny likeness of Satyavan, no bigger than a thumb.

Satyavan's breathing stopped.

Yama placed the likeness inside his robe. "Happiness awaits your husband in my kingdom. Satyavan is a man of great virtue."

Then Yama turned and headed south, back to his domain.

Savitri rose and started after him.

The Magic Brocade • By Aaron Shepard

One day, Chen came in to find the loom empty and the widow sobbing. "What's wrong, Mother?" he asked in alarm.

She looked at him tearfully. "I finished it."

The brocade was laid out on the floor. And there it all was—the palace reaching to the sky, the beautiful gardens, the lovely fairy ladies.

"It looks so real," said Chen in amazement. "I feel like I could step into it!"

Just then, a sudden wind whipped through the cottage. It lifted the brocade, blew it out the window, and carried it through the air. The widow and her son rushed outside, only to watch the brocade disappear into the east.

"It's gone!" cried the widow, and she fainted away.

Chen carried her to her bed and sat beside her for many hours. At last her eyes opened.

"Chen," she said weakly, "you must find the brocade and bring it back."

"Don't worry, Mother. I'll go at once."

Chen gathered a few things and started to the east. He walked for hours, then days, then weeks. But there was no sign of the brocade.

One day, Chen came upon a lonely hut. Sitting by the door was an old, leather-skinned woman smoking a pipe. A horse was grazing nearby.

"Hello, deary," said the woman. "What brings you so far from home?"

"I'm looking for my mother's brocade. The wind carried it to the east."

"Ah, yes," said the woman. "The brocade of Sun Palace! Well, that wind was sent by the fairy ladies of the palace itself. They're using the brocade as a pattern for their weaving."

"But my mother will die without it!"

"Well, then, you had best get it back! But you won't get to Sun Palace by foot, so you'd better ride my horse. It will show you the way."

"Thank you!" said Chen.

"Oh, don't thank me yet, deary. Between here and there, you must pass through the flames of Fiery Mountain. If you make a single sound of complaint, you'll be burnt to ashes. After that, you must cross the Icy Sea. The smallest word of discontent, and you'll be frozen solid. Do you still want to go?"

"I must get back my mother's brocade."

"Good boy. Take the horse and go."

The Enchanted Storks • By Aaron Shepard

Reaching the edge of the city, the Calif and his Vizier strolled through the parks and orchards beyond. At last they stopped to rest by a quiet lake.

"I wonder if my new box holds any snuff," said the Calif.

He opened the tiny box and found it filled with the pungent powder. "But what is this?" he said, pulling a piece of parchment from the underside of the lid.

The Vizier craned his neck to see. "What does it say, Glorious Lord?"

The Calif read,

> A sniff of snuff, for wings to soar.
> *Casalavair* for hands once more.

"Why, I believe the snuff is magic!" said the Calif. He looked longingly at the sky. "I have always wanted to see my city from the air."

"Perhaps we should be cautious," said the Vizier. "What if the charm fails to change us back?"

"If the snuff works, then surely the magic word will too," said the Calif. "Come, let us try our luck!"

He held out the box, and each took a pinch of snuff. Then together they inhaled the powder.

A flurry of wings, beaks, and feathers—and there in place of the Calif and his Vizier stood two storks.

"Wonderful!" the Calif said, snapping and clattering his beak—for that is how storks talk. A human would have heard only *Calap! Calap!* But since both the Calif and his Vizier were now birds, Ali ben Manzar understood perfectly.

Calap! Calap! "Quite amazing!" replied the Vizier.

Calap! Calap! "Let us test our wings!" said the Calif.

Soon they soared above the streets, canals, bridges, and clay-brick buildings of Bagdad. In courtyard and bazaar, people bought and sold, worked and rested, fought and prayed, stole and chased, kissed and parted, laughed and wept.

"Truly," said the Calif, "a stork knows more of this city than the Calif himself."

Master Maid • By Aaron Shepard

When the troll had gone, Leif said to himself, "Not look through the house? Why, that's just what I want to do!"

So Leif went through all the rooms till he came to the kitchen. And there stirring a big iron pot was the loveliest maiden he had ever seen.

"Good Lord!" cried the girl. "What are you doing here?"

"I've just got a job with the troll," said Leif.

"Then heaven help you get out of it!" said the girl. "Weren't you warned about working here?"

"I was," said Leif, "but I'm glad I came anyway, else I never would have met you!"

Well, the girl liked *that* answer, so they sat down to chat. They talked and talked and talked some more, and before the day was done, he held her hand in his.

Then the girl asked, "What did the troll tell you to do today?"

"Something easy," said Leif. "I've only to clear the dung from the stable."

"Easy to say!" said the girl. "But if you use the pitchfork the ordinary way, ten forkfuls will fly in for every one you throw out! Now, here's what you must do. Turn the pitchfork around and shovel with the handle. Then the dung will fly out by itself."

Leif went out to the stable and took up the pitchfork. But he said to himself, "That can't be true, what she told me," and he shoveled the ordinary way. Within moments, he was up to his neck in dung.

"I guess her way wouldn't hurt to try," he said. So he turned the pitchfork around and shoveled with the handle. In no time at all, the dung was all out, and the stable looked like he had scrubbed it.

As Leif started back to the house, the troll came up with the goats.

"Is the stable clean?" asked the troll.

"Tight and tidy!" said Leif, and he showed it to him.

"You never figured this out for yourself!" the troll said. "Have you been talking to my Master Maid?"

"Master Maid?" said Leif. "Now, what sort of thing might that be, sir?"

"You'll find out soon enough," said the troll.

Forty Fortunes • By Aaron Shepard

Taken from the picture book *Forty Fortunes: A Tale of Iran,* told by Aaron Shepard, illustrated by Alisher Dianov, Clarion, 1999. Copyright © 1997, 1999, 2004 Aaron Shepard. May be copied for any noncommercial purpose. *Ahmed* is pronounced "AH-med." *Jamell* is pronounced "ja-MEL." More at **www.aaronshep.com**.

That evening, when Ahmed handed his wife his wages for the day, she said, "Look at these few measly coins! I won't put up with this any longer. Tomorrow you'll sit in the marketplace and be a diviner!"

"Jamell, are you insane?" said Ahmed. "What do I know about fortunetelling?"

"You don't need to know a thing," said Jamell. "When anyone brings you a question, you just throw the dice and mumble something that sounds wise. It's either that, or I go home to the house of my father!"

So the next day, Ahmed sold his shovel and his pick and bought the dice and the board and the robe of a fortuneteller. Then he sat in the marketplace near the public bath.

Hardly had he gotten settled when there ran up to him the wife of one of the King's ministers.

"Diviner, you must help me! I wore my most precious ring to the bath today, and now it's missing. Please, tell me where it is!"

Ahmed gulped and cast the dice. As he desperately searched for something wise to say, he happened to glance up at the lady's cloak. There he spied a small hole, and showing through the hole, a bit of her naked arm.

Of course, this was quite improper for a respectable lady, so Ahmed leaned forward and whispered urgently, "Madam, I see a hole."

"A what?" asked the lady, leaning closer.

"A hole! A hole!"

The lady brightened. "Of course! A hole!"

She rushed back to the bath and found the hole in the wall where she had hidden her ring for safekeeping and forgotten it. Then she came back to Ahmed.

"God be praised!" she said. "You knew right where it was!" And to Ahmed's amazement, she gave him a gold coin.

That evening, when Jamell saw the coin and heard the story, she said, "You see? There's nothing to it!"

"God was merciful today," said Ahmed, "but I dare not test Him again!"

"Nonsense," said Jamell. "If you want to keep your wife, you'll be back in the marketplace tomorrow."

The Legend of Slappy Hooper • By Aaron Shepard

Taken from the picture book *The Legend of Slappy Hooper: An American Tall Tale,* told by Aaron Shepard, illustrated by Toni Goffe, Scribners/Atheneum, 1993. Copyright © 1993, 1997, 2004 Aaron Shepard. May be copied for any noncommercial purpose. More at **www.aaronshep.com**.

After that, no one on earth would hire Slappy. It looked as if his sign-painting days were done.

Slappy felt so low, he made up his mind to throw his paint kit in the river. He dragged it onto the tallest bridge in town and was just about to chuck it, when a voice thundered out beside him.

"Don't dump that gear, Slappy Hooper. You're going to need it!"

Right next to Slappy stood a man almost as big as Slappy himself. He wore a paint-splotched white coverall and a cap with two little angel wings sticking out. He carried an eight-inch brush.

"Who are *you*?" said Slappy.

"I'm Michael, from the Heavenly Sign Company," thundered the man. "The Boss has had an eye on you for some time, Slappy, and He likes your work. He's got a job for you—if you don't mind working in the rain."

"Tell me about it," said Slappy.

"We need someone to paint a rainbow this Wednesday," said Michael. "Most of the time, we handle all the rainbows ourselves. But it's going to rain in a bunch of places Wednesday, and we could sure use some help."

"I'm your man," said Slappy.

That Wednesday morning, Slappy rented a cannon and set it in a big cow pasture. He tied two ropes to his scaffold, then ran the other ends through a couple of skyhooks. Then he loaded the skyhooks in the cannon and shot them straight up.

Sure enough, the skyhooks caught on the sky.

Slappy felt the first raindrops. He piled all his paints and brushes onto his scaffold, climbed on, and hoisted himself up, up, and up!

He kept going till he was just under the clouds. Then he tied his ropes and started to paint.

Slip! slop! slap!

Slappy had only just finished, when the sun popped through the clouds and lit up what he'd done.

There never was a finer rainbow! It had every color you could imagine, each one blending perfectly with the next. And not a brush stroke in sight.

The Gifts of Wali Dad • By Aaron Shepard

The next day, Wali Dad loaded the money into a sack and carried it to a jeweler in the marketplace. He exchanged all his coins for a lovely gold bracelet.

Then Wali Dad visited the home of a traveling merchant.

"Tell me," said Wali Dad, "in all the world, who is the noblest lady?"

"Without doubt," said the merchant, "it is the young queen of Khaistan. I often visit her palace, just three days' journey to the east."

"Do me a kindness," said Wali Dad. "The next time you pass that way, give her this little bracelet, with my compliments."

The merchant was astonished, but he agreed to do what the ragged grass-cutter asked.

Soon after, the merchant found himself at the palace of the queen of Khaistan. He presented the bracelet to her as a gift from Wali Dad.

"How lovely!" she said, admiring the bracelet. "Your friend must accept a gift in return. My servants will load a camel with the finest silks."

When the merchant arrived back home, he brought the silks to the hut of Wali Dad. "Oh, no!" said the grass-cutter. "This is worse than before! What am I to do with such finery?"

"Perhaps," said the merchant, "you could give it to someone else."

Wali Dad thought for a moment. "Tell me," he said, "in all the world, who is the noblest man?"

"That is simple," said the merchant. "It is the young king of Nekabad. His palace, too, I often visit, just three days' journey to the west."

"Then do me another kindness," begged Wali Dad. "On your next trip there, give him these silks, with my compliments."

The merchant was amused, but he agreed. On his next journey, he presented the silks to the king of Nekabad. "A splendid gift!" said the king, admiring the silks. "In return, your friend must have twelve of my finest horses."

So the merchant brought the king's horses to Wali Dad. "This grows worse and worse!" declared the old man. "What could I do with twelve horses?"

But after a moment Wali Dad said, "I know who should have such a gift. I beg you, keep two horses for yourself, and take the rest to the queen of Khaistan!"

More Than a Match • By Aaron Shepard

With a cart and horse loaned by the King, the Wise One drove out till he came to the giant, who was now dressed up like a Wise One.

The giant shouted,

"None shall pass without a fight.
Choose your weapon, dark or light.
I'll more than match you, wrong or right!"

"Well!" said the Wise One. "I shall have to think on this!" And so saying, he settled himself to ponder.

The giant stood stone still.

After a while, the Wise One's stomach grumbled. He reached into his bag for a loaf of brown bread and broke off a piece. He was about to bite into it when he heard a growl from the stomach of the giant.

"Perhaps you too are hungry," said the Wise One pleasantly. He held out the piece of bread. "Would you care to share my humble repast?"

"So!" cried the giant. "You try to conquer me with kindness! But now I'll more than match you."

Almost faster than the Wise One could see, the giant took from his own bag a table and chair and all manner of tasty, wholesome dishes fit for a Wise One—grains, cheeses, vegetables, fruits. Then before the Wise One could look twice, the giant stood there again, solid as rock and blocking the road.

"So *that's* the way of it," murmured the Wise One.

He got down from the cart and sat at the table to enjoy the giant's offering. When he'd eaten enough to satisfy his hunger, and a little more, he leaned back contentedly and gazed thoughtfully at the giant.

"I should like you to know a little about me. I live in a cottage in a forest outside the city of Here. And though I make no such claim for myself, others call me the Wise One."

The giant bellowed, "Another contest! But you won't win, because now I'll tell you even more about *me*. I have no name, for my father is the wind, and my mother is a curved mirror. Like any mirror, I show only what I see, and I have no power or skill but what you choose."

Peddler Polly and the Story Stealer • By Aaron Shepard

"Stop the Swap!" cried Mayor Bigwig. "We can't afford to lose any more stories. It's the end of storytelling in Taletown!"

As excited talk filled the room, Peddler Polly thought she heard a cackle out the window. She looked and saw a man with a topcoat and top hat hurry away from the building. He carried a large wooden box covered with switches, knobs, and dials, with a long hose attached to it.

"It's Dr. Spellbinder!" said Peddler Polly. "I'd better look into this."

Peddler Polly hastened from the hall. She followed Dr. Spellbinder from a distance as he left the town and made his way into the hills.

At last Dr. Spellbinder disappeared through the mouth of a cave. Peddler Polly followed him in and stopped in astonishment. The huge cave was filled with mechanisms and contraptions, all of them noisily pulling or pushing or pulsing or pounding.

Dr. Spellbinder stood at a workbench covered with Storyboxes and other strange devices. He set down the big box he was carrying and patted it fondly.

"Three more stories to put in my Storyboxes!" he said. "And all thanks to my brilliant invention, the Spellbinder Story Sucker. Soon I'll steal all the stories in the world! Then *everyone* will need a Storybox, and I'll be rich, *rich,* RICH."

"Not if *I* can help it!" said Peddler Polly.

Dr. Spellbinder spun around. "Peddler Polly! What are *you* doing here?"

"Putting an end to your evil plans, Spellbinder!"

"You'll never stop me, Peddler Polly!" Then Dr. Spellbinder grabbed the Story Sucker and sprinted from the cave.

Down the hill sped Dr. Spellbinder, while Peddler Polly puffed in pursuit. Without the Story Sucker, Peddler Polly was faster.

"You won't catch me so easily," yelled Dr. Spellbinder. He lifted the lid on the Story Sucker and reached in. "See how you like *this* story, Peddler Polly."

He threw something behind him. There was a flash of light, and out of nowhere a huge crowd of children appeared, coming uphill toward Peddler Polly. They were led by a man in a many-colored costume, playing on a pipe.

"Well, I'll be!" said Peddler Polly as she pushed past the startled man and pressed through the crowd of mesmerized children. "It's a catchy tune, kids, but I wouldn't follow a pied piper!"

Kings for Breakfast! • By Aaron Shepard

Taken from the story "Kings for Breakfast!: A Hindu Legend," told by Aaron Shepard. Copyright © 1993, 2004 Aaron Shepard. May be copied for any noncommercial purpose. *Vikram* is pronounced "VIK-rum." *Karna* is pronounced "KAR-na." More at **www.aaronshep.com**.

One day, while Vikram was strolling through his palace garden, two snow-white geese landed at his feet.

"Good King Vikram, we are starving!" cried the gander. "We beg you to feed us!"

"Certainly," said Vikram. "I will send for seed at once."

"We cannot eat seed," said the female. "We come from a sacred lake, high in the mountains of the north. There, we eat only fresh pearls."

"Then pearls it shall be," said Vikram. He sent for a basket of his finest pearls and fed the geese from his hand.

Each morning, Vikram fed the geese. But one morning, the gander noticed that one of the pearls was pierced.

"Look!" he cried to his mate. "These pearls are not fresh!"

"Not even King Vikram can feed us forever," she said. "Let us fly elsewhere."

Before Vikram could protest, the geese rose into the air. But as they soared, they cried, "Thanks, thanks to Vikram, the most generous king of all!"

The geese flew on, singing Vikram's praises. On their way, they passed over the palace of King Karna.

When the king heard their song, he said, "Why is Vikram praised even by the birds? Surely he's no more generous than I!" And he sent his royal hunter to trap the geese where they landed.

The geese were brought in a cage before King Karna. He asked them, "Why do you call Vikram the most generous king of all?"

"He fed us pearls from his hand," said the gander.

"But I give away a hundred pounds of gold each day!" said the king. "Am I not as generous as Vikram?"

The female said, "King Vikram would never imprison the innocent."

King Karna took a handful of pearls and opened the cage door to reach in. But the female pushed past and flew out the window.

Swiftly the goose flew back to Vikram and landed breathless at his feet. "Good King Vikram," she said, "you must help us! My husband is a prisoner!"

Vikram listened to her story. "Rest easy, dear friend," he said. "I will rescue your mate."

The Boy Who Wanted the Willies • By Aaron Shepard

It was midnight when Hans reached the castle. The towers cast eerie shadows under the full moon. The drawbridge lowered itself at Hans's feet. *Creeeeeeeeeeeek.*

"Seems like a friendly place!" said Hans.

As Hans entered the great hall, a fire sprang to life in the huge fireplace. Hans pulled up a chair and settled himself to wait.

"Now I'm *sure* to get the willies," he said.

The clock in the great hall struck one. *Bong.*

"Velcome!" boomed a voice behind him.

Hans looked around and saw two men playing cards. One had a long, black cloak, and the other had a furry face.

"Vould you care to join our game?" asked the man in the cloak. "It's been so long since ve had anyvun to play vith."

"Certainly," said Hans, taking a seat. "It will pass the time while I'm waiting for the willies!"

"I vill explain the rules," said the cloaked man. "If my furry friend vins, he vill rip you to shreds. If I vin, I vill drink your blood. If you vin, ve vill let you live."

"Sounds fair to me!" said Hans.

The furry man snarled and dealt the cards. They played for almost an hour. In the end, the cloaked man won.

"I vant to drink your blood!" he said, moving closer to Hans and showing two long, pointy teeth.

"I think you cheated," Hans said. He reached for the pointy teeth and broke them off—*Snap!*

"YEEE-OWWWWWWWW!" howled the man as he ran from the room.

The furry man roared and leaped at Hans, but Hans sprang away and the man flew past—right out an open window. A piercing scream ended in a dull *thud.*

Hans settled himself again before the fire. "I enjoyed the game," he said, "but when do I get the willies?"

The clock struck two. *Bong. Bong.*

The Magic of Mushkil Gusha • By Aaron Shepard

Next morning, the woodcutter awoke while it was still dark. He told himself, "I might as well go out right now and get another big load of wood. Then I can sell twice as much and buy even more date cakes."

So he left his load and went back to the desert to gather more bushes. But again he took longer than he meant to, and when he got back, it was dark and the door was bolted. So again he had to sleep on the doorstep.

He awoke once more before dawn. "There's no sense wasting a day," he said. "I'll go back out for one more big load. How many date cakes we'll have then!"

But yet again he took too long, and yet again the door was bolted when he got back.

The woodcutter sank to the doorstep and wept.

"What's wrong, old man?"

He looked up to see a dervish in a long green robe and a tall green cap.

"Holy sir, for three days I have gone out to gather thorn bushes, and for three days I have come home too late to get into my house. And in all that time, I've had nothing to eat."

"What night is this, old man?"

The woodcutter said, "Why, Friday eve, of course."

"That's right. It's the eve of our holy day. And that's the time of Mushkil Gusha."

"Mushkil Gusha?" said the woodcutter.

"That's right, old man—the 'Remover of Difficulties.'"

The holy man took some roasted chickpeas and raisins from his pouch and handed them to the woodcutter. "Here, share this with me."

"Thank you, sir!"

"You may not know it," the dervish went on, "but Mushkil Gusha is already helping you. If you want your good fortune to continue, here's what you must do: Every Friday eve, find someone in need. Then share what you have, and tell a tale of Mushkil Gusha. That way, you both will be helped."

And with that, the holy man vanished.

The Millionaire Miser • By Aaron Shepard

Sushil was a miser. Though his treasure house was full, he was too stingy to give away even the smallest coin. And since food cost money, he ate almost nothing, and starved his family and servants besides.

One morning, as Sushil took his daily walk through town, he saw a young boy eating a sweet rice dumpling. Sushil's mouth watered as he made his way home.

"If only I could ask my wife to make me a sweet dumpling," he said to himself. "But if *I* wanted one, so would my wife. And if my wife wanted one, so would the children. And if the children wanted one, so would the servants. So I had better just keep quiet."

When Sushil arrived home, he said nothing about a dumpling. But he wanted one so badly, he felt weak. His legs shook, and he had to go to bed.

His wife, Nirmala, came to him. She asked, "What is wrong, my husband?"

Sushil lay groaning and clenched his teeth.

"Is there something you want?" said Nirmala.

Sushil's face grew red, then purple. At last he squeaked, "I would like a sweet rice dumpling."

"That is no problem," said Nirmala. "We are wealthy enough. Why, I will make sweet dumplings for the whole town!"

Sushil gasped in horror. "You will make a pauper of me!"

"Well then," said Nirmala, "I will make dumplings for our family and servants."

"Why would the servants need any?" said Sushil.

"Then I will make them for us and the children."

"I am sure the children can do without."

"Then I will make one for you and one for me."

"Why would *you* want one?" said Sushil.

Nirmala sighed and went out, and returned after a while with a single sweet dumpling. Then she looked on as Sushil, moaning with delight, devoured every crumb.

The Lady of Stavoren • By Aaron Shepard

At long last, the Captain's ship was sighted entering the harbor. The people of Stavoren streamed to the dock. When the Lady arrived, dressed in her finest, they made way.

The Captain's ship was just docking. "My Lady," he called, "I have brought what you desired! The most precious thing in the world!"

"What is it, my Captain?" called back the Lady, barely able to hold in her excitement.

"I visited many ports in many lands," the Captain said. "I saw many wonderful things. None could I say was the most precious of all. But at last, in the city of Danzig, I came across it. Then I laughed at myself! I should have known it from the first!"

"But what is it?" said the Lady impatiently.

"Wheat!" cried the Captain. "My ship is filled with wheat!"

"Wheat?" said the Lady. Her face grew white. Behind her, she heard murmurs from the crowd, and laughing. "Did you say *wheat*?"

"Yes, dear Lady!" said the Captain joyously. "What could be more precious, more valuable, than wheat? Without our daily bread, what good are all the treasures of the world?"

The Lady was silent for a moment, listening to the whispers and snickers of the crowd. "And this wheat belongs to me, to do with as I like?"

"Yes, my love! It is my wedding gift to you!"

"Then," said the Lady, "pour it into the harbor."

"What?" Now the Captain's own face was white.

"Pour it into the harbor! Every grain of it!"

Murmurs of horror and approval both rose behind her.

"My Lady," said the Captain, "please consider what you say. There is wheat enough here to feed a city! If you have no use for it, then give it to the poor and hungry. After all, you too may someday be in need."

"I?" shrieked the Lady. "In need?"

She plucked from her finger the ruby ring the Captain had given her and held it high. "This ring will return to my hand before I am ever in need."

With all her might, she flung it far into the harbor.

The Hidden One • By Aaron Shepard

Little Scarface sat huddled for a long time, listening to her sister howl and sob. Then she rose and said again, "It is my turn to visit the Hidden One."

Her sister stopped crying and stared in amazement.

Little Scarface went to her father's chest and took out an old pair of moccasins. She put them on her own small feet.

Then she went out into the woods. She chose a birch tree and carefully stripped off the bark in a single sheet. From this she made a suit of clothes, which she put on in place of her rags.

Then she started back through the village.

"Look at Little Scarface!" yelled a boy. "She's dressed like a tree!"

"Hey, Little Scarface," a young man called, "are those moccasins big enough for you?"

"I don't believe it!" an old woman said. "She's on her way to the Hidden One!"

"Little Scarface," called a young woman, "did you burn yourself and cut off your hair to look pretty for him?"

Ignoring their taunts and laughter, Little Scarface walked on till she reached the wigwam at the village edge.

The Patient One regarded the young woman with surprise, but she told her, "You are welcome."

Little Scarface helped prepare the evening meal. When the sun was nearly down, the Patient One led her to the lake.

"My brother comes," the Patient One told her. "Do you see him?"

Little Scarface gazed along the shore. "I'm not sure . . . ."

Then her eyes lit in wonder. "Yes, I see him! But how can there be such a one?"

The Patient One looked at her curiously. "What is his shoulder strap?"

"His shoulder strap is . . . is the Rainbow!"

The Patient One's eyes grew wide. "And his bowstring?"

"His bowstring is . . . the Milky Way!"

The Patient One smiled. "Let us return."

The Four Puppets • By Aaron Shepard

The next day took Aung into the mountains, and at sunset he left the road
and camped a little way up the mountainside. When he awoke the next morning,
he saw a caravan coming along the road below. A dozen bullock carts were piled
high with costly goods.

"That caravan must belong to some rich merchant," Aung told himself.
"I wish I had wealth like that."

Then he had a thought. He turned to the puppet of the green-faced ogre.
"Tell me, how can I gain such riches?"

Aung watched in wonder as the puppet left the pole and grew to life size.
"If you have strength," boomed the ogre, "you can take whatever you like. Watch
this!" He stamped his foot and the earth shook.

"Wait!" said Aung. But it was too late. Just below them, dirt and rocks
broke loose in a landslide. It rushed down the mountain and blocked the road.
The terrified drivers jumped from their carts and ran off.

"You see?" said the ogre.

"Is it really that easy?" said Aung, in a daze.

He hurried down to the carts and rushed from one to another, gaping
at the heaps of rich fabrics and piles of precious metals. "And all of it's mine!"
he cried.

Just then, Aung heard a sob. Lying huddled in one of the carts was a lovely
young woman his own age. She cried and shivered in fear.

"I won't hurt you," said Aung gently. "Who are you?"

"My name is Mala," she said in a small voice. "My father is the owner of
this caravan. We were on our way to meet him."

All at once, Aung knew he was in love. He wanted to keep Mala with him
forever. "Don't worry," he said. "I'll take you with me and care for you."

Mala sat up angrily. "Go ahead! Take me, like you're taking everything
else! But you're just a thief, and I'll never, ever speak to you!"

Aung was shocked. Was he really just a thief? He didn't know what to say.

The ogre came up beside him then. "Don't listen to her. She'll change
her mind—and anyway, the important thing is you got what you wanted. Now,
let's go."

The Story Spirits • By Aaron Shepard

At last the wedding day arrived. In the early morning, Dong Chin and his father made ready to go to the bride's house for the ceremony. Everyone bustled about to help and to prepare for the celebration the next day, when the bride would be brought home.

Pak the servant was busy like everyone else. But as he rushed around, he happened to pass outside Dong Chin's room. To his surprise, he heard a murmur of many voices.

"That's strange," he said to himself. "The young master isn't in there now, and no one else should be either."

He went up to the paper window, carefully poked a small hole, and peeked through. Then he gasped.

The air was teeming with spirits—hundreds of them! Over, under, and around each other they swarmed. There were so many, they barely had room to fly, and they didn't look one bit happy!

"Silence!" called one of the spirits. "Stop talking all at once, or we'll never get anywhere."

The murmur died away. "That's right," said another spirit. "The boy's wedding is today, and we have to decide what to do."

"We must have revenge!" said another. "He has to be punished for keeping us stories all stuck here."

Pak gasped again. "It's the stories!" he said in wonder. "The ones that had to stay in the room!"

"Yes, he must be punished," said another spirit. "But how?"

"I have an idea," said another. "I'm a story that has a poisoned well in it. Why don't I put my well by the road? If he drinks the water, he'll be deathly ill."

"Wonderful!" said another. "I'm a story with poisoned strawberries in it. I'll set them farther down the road, in case he doesn't drink."

"Good thinking!" said another. "I'm a story with a red-hot poker. I'll put it in the cushion he steps onto at the bride's house—in case he neither eats nor drinks on the way. It will burn him terribly!"

"That should do it," said still another. "But in case he escapes you all, I'll be ready. I'm a story with a deadly snake. I'll hide it under the sleeping mat of the bride. When they go to bed, it will bite and kill them both!"

The Wicked Girl • By Aaron Shepard

There was once a merchant who set out with his wife on a pilgrimage to Mecca. Their daughter, though, they left at home, with an Arab slave girl to keep her company.

One evening quite late, the merchant's daughter and the Arab girl were singing and laughing and dancing about in the upstairs apartment. By accident, the Arab girl knocked over the oil lamp, leaving the young ladies in darkness.

"What should we do?" said the merchant's daughter. "It's too late to rouse the servants."

"I'll go out and find a light," said the Arab girl.

"But we're locked in!" said the merchant's daughter.

"The window's open," said the Arab girl.

So they knotted some bed sheets together and lowered them from the window. Then the Arab girl took a basket and climbed down.

She walked down the street till she came to a restaurant still open. The customers had all gone, but a handsome young man was in the kitchen, cleaning up and preparing for the next day. On the table were dishes piled high with kebabs, dolma, pilaf, and baklava.

"May I come in?" said the Arab girl prettily.

The young man, who owned the restaurant, cast an eye on the lovely young lady. "Please sit down!" he said.

As the two of them chatted, the young man moved closer and closer to the Arab girl. She was almost in reach when she asked him, "What's in those huge crocks?"

"One has olive oil, one has clarified butter, and one has honey."

"Honey?" she said. "What's that?"

"Surely you've had honey before!"

"Never! Please give me a taste."

So the young man took off the lid and leaned into the crock to spoon some out. The Arab girl came up behind and lifted his feet, so he slid head first into the honey. Then she quickly loaded her basket with dishes of food, grabbed an oil lamp, and ran off.

The young man came out of the honey dripping and sputtering. "Ooh, that Arab girl! If I ever catch her, I'll get her good!"

Lars, My Lad! • By Aaron Shepard

There was once a young duke who was down on his luck. He'd started with a good deal of money and a great many friends, but when his money ran out, his friends did too.

And so he found himself one night, ragged, cold, and starved, wandering through a lonely forest. He had nearly given up finding shelter for the night, when he came upon a deserted, ramshackle hut.

"It's better than sleeping on the ground," he said.

The duke went in, and there found nothing but a large chest, standing in the middle of the hut. Hoping it held some scraps of food, he unlatched it and lifted the lid.

Inside was another chest. He heaved out that one and opened it also, but found only another chest within. This too he pulled out and opened, but found still another chest inside it.

"Whatever's in here must be of great value, to be tucked away so well," he said, and he kept on taking out and opening chests, until the floor was quite covered by them.

Finally he came to a tiny box, and inside he found a scrap of paper.

"Is that all?" snorted the duke, and he was about to crumple and toss it aside, when he noticed some words written on it. They were so faded, he could hardly make them out.

"Lars . . . my . . . lad."

"Master, what do you wish?"

The duke jumped in surprise. But when he looked around him, he could not see who had spoken.

"Let's try that again," said the duke, and holding the paper before him, he read, "Lars, my lad!"

"Master, what do you wish?"

The duke could still see no one, but he had an idea it didn't matter.

"Bring me a table," he said, "and set it with the richest feast anyone ever sat down to."

A whisk, a whir, and a whoosh, and there in the hut was a banquet table such as the duke had never seen. He settled himself down and never stopped eating till he had made up for all his days of hunger.

I Know What I Know • By Aaron Shepard

Once there was a man named Ulf who had three grown-up daughters. Each had married a troll and gone to live inside a hill.

Ulf had not seen any of them since their weddings. One day he decided to visit the eldest. He walked till he came to the hill where she lived.

A door in the hillside flew open. "Welcome!" said his daughter, and she let him in.

"Husband, look!" she told the troll. "My father's here! Will you go buy some meat for the stew?"

"Why buy what is already owned?" said the troll.

He picked up a mallet and hit himself on the back of the head. *Thunk!* His head flew off into the stew pot, and a new head grew on his shoulders.

"Ah!" said Ulf.

When he got home, he told his wife, "I have learned something wonderful!"

"What have you learned?" she asked.

But Ulf just smiled and said, "I know what I know."

A few days later, Ulf's wife told him, "We need meat for the stew. Will you go buy some?"

"Why buy what is already owned?" said Ulf. He picked up a mallet and knocked himself on the back of the head. *Thunk!*

"Oof!" said Ulf. He fell senseless to the floor.

When he came to, his wife said, "Husband, why in the world did you hit yourself?"

"Never mind!" said Ulf grumpily. "I know what I know!"

Ulf spent the next few days in bed. When the bump on his head had gone down, he decided to visit his middle daughter. He walked till he came to the hill where she lived.

A door in the hill flew open. "Welcome!" said his daughter. "Husband, look! My father's here! Will you go buy some candles for the table?"

"Why go far for what is near?" said the troll.

He put his hand in the fire. *Sssss.* When he pulled it out, his fingers were lit like candles and made the room quite bright.

"Oh!" said Ulf.

Part 4 ~ Other RT Resources

Books and Articles

Stories on Stage: Scripts for Reader's Theater, by Aaron Shepard, H. W. Wilson, 1993; Shepard Publications, 2005. The premier collection of reader's theater scripts, with adaptations of stories by a variety of authors. Mostly for ages 8 to 15. (The H. W. Wilson edition included additional scripts for higher ages.)

Folktales on Stage: 16 Scripts for Reader's Theater (or Readers Theatre) From Folk and Fairy Tales of the World, by Aaron Shepard, Shepard Publications, 2004. Scripts based on my own picture books and stories. Mostly for ages 8 to 15.

Presenting Reader's Theater: Plays and Poems to Read Aloud, by Caroline Feller Bauer, H. W. Wilson, 1987. Scripts adapted from a variety of children's authors, plus advice. Primary grades. Best ordering is direct from the publisher, at www.hwwilson.com/print/readtheater.htm.

From the Page to the Stage: The Educator's Complete Guide to Readers Theatre, by Shirlee Sloyer, Teacher Ideas Press, 2003. Just what the subtitle says, plus sample scripts. Elementary and middle grades.

Institute Book of Readers Theatre: A Practical Guide for School, Theater, & Community, by William Adams, Institute for Readers Theatre, 2003. A university-level textbook from a bastion and pioneer of reader's theater. The most comprehensive treatment of reader's theater available. Best ordering is at www.readerstheatreinstitute.com.

Readers Theatre for Beginning Readers, by Suzanne I. Barchers, Teacher Ideas Press, 1993. Twenty-four scripts of folktales and fables from around the world, plus tips on reader's theater in the classroom. Grades 1–4. One of many reader's theater titles by this author.

Frantic Frogs and Other Frankly Fractured Folktales for Readers Theatre, by Anthony D. Fredericks, Teacher Ideas Press, 1993. Fiercely funny flummery for grades 4–8. Kids love this kind of stuff! One of many reader's theater titles by this author.

Playbooks for Young Readers by Aaron and ***Playbooks for Tween Readers by Aaron,*** adapted from tales told by Aaron Shepard, Playbooks, Laguna Hills, California, 2002. These are publisher adaptations of three each of my scripts into Playbook format, which features illustrations, color-coding, and diverse reading levels for small groups of students or for families. For ages 5–10 and 8–13, respectively. Available in both printed and electronic formats. Best ordering is direct from the publisher, at www.eplaybooks.com.

Multicultural Folktales for the Feltboard and Readers' Theater, by Judy Sierra, Oryx, 1996. Short and simple scripts by a popular children's author. Grades 3–8.

Great Moments in Science: Experiments and Readers Theatre, by Kendall Haven, Teacher Ideas Press, 1996. Combines scripts about famous scientists with experiments that demonstrate the principles they discovered. Grades 4–9.

Readers Theatre Strategies in the Elementary Classroom, 1990, and ***Readers Theatre Strategies in the Middle and Junior High Classroom,*** 1997, by Lois Walker, Take Part Productions. Include tips on several different styles of reader's theater, plus ways to tie in to storytelling, writing, and creative drama. Lois is a leading proponent of reader's theater in Canada, as well as a workshop leader, script publisher, and children's television producer.

Learning with Readers Theatre: Building Connections, by Neill Dixon, Anne Davies, and Colleen Politano, Peguis, 1996. A comprehensive approach to using reader's theater in the classroom, from scripting to performance. Neill Dixon is the head of Readers Theatre International in Canada.

Readers Theatre Handbook: A Dramatic Approach to Literature, by Leslie Irene Coger and Melvin R. White, Scott, Foresman, 1982. Techniques and some scripts, drawn from the early days of reader's theater. College.

Be a Mime!, by Mark Stolzenberg, Sterling, 1991 (originally published as *Exploring Mime*). A good beginning book on mime techniques. A bit of mime can do wonders for reader's theater!

"The Power of Reader's Theater," by Jennifer O. Prescott, *Instructor*, Jan.–Feb. 2003. Encouragement and advice from teachers using RT.

"Reader's Theater: A Reason to Read Aloud," by Cara Bafile, Education World, www.educationworld.com. Tips from experts, including many promoters of my own RT resources.

Online Resources

Web Sites

Aaron Shepard's RT Page. My own online resources for reader's theater, including the acclaimed series of free downloadable scripts Reader's Theater Editions. Check at this site for updates and additional resource listings.

> www.aaronshep.com/rt

Readers Theatre Digest. An online journal of RT, with articles, interviews, and reviews, published by Robert Demers.

> www.readerstheatredigest.com

Teaching Heart ~ Reader's Theater Scripts and Plays. A nice collection of links by Colleen Gallagher to scripts around the Web (including some of mine).

> www.teachingheart.net/readerstheater.htm

Literacy Connections ~ Readers' Theater. Another fine collection of links.

> www.literacyconnections.com/ReadersTheater.html

Email Lists

ReadersTheater. A list founded by myself and now owned by Robert Demers.

> groups.yahoo.com/group/ReadersTheater

Suppliers

All addresses are U.S. unless noted.

Readers Theatre Script Service. Sells individual scripts with tips on staging. Part of the Institute for Readers Theatre headed by William Adams of San Diego State University.

> P. O. Box 17193
> San Diego, CA 92177
> 619-276-1948
> www.readerstheatreinstitute.com

Scripts for Schools. Scripts from Lois Walker for a wide range of grades, in ready-to-use packets.

> Box 86756
> North Vancouver, BC V7L 4L3 CANADA
> 604-925-1989
> www.scriptsforschools.com

Storycart Press. Script sets and collections for young readers from Suzanne Barchers. The Web site includes free sample scripts.

> 381 Rock Road East
> Lambertville, NJ 08530
> 203-975-8465
> www.storycart.com

Playbooks. Reader's theater scripts for classroom or family use, illustrated and with individual parts color-coded and graded for reading level. Includes their adaptations of some of my own scripts.

> 23232 Peralta Dr, #201
> Laguna Hills, CA 92653
> 800-375-2926
> www.eplaybooks.com

Training

All addresses are U.S. unless noted.

Institute for Readers Theatre. Leads workshops, and holds annual seminars in exotic locales. Headed by William Adams of San Diego State University.

> P. O. Box 17193
> San Diego, CA 92177
> 619-276-1948
> www.readerstheatreinstitute.com

Chamber Readers. A top-rank performance group that can lead workshops on request.

> P.O. Box 103
> Bayside, CA 95524
> 707-725-2677

Author Online!

For more reader's theater, visit
Aaron Shepard's RT Page at

www.aaronshep.com/rt

Index

Aaron Shepard's RT Page, 10, 12, 102
action (in story or script), 41, 47, 49, 50, 52, 54, 55
adapting. *See* scripts and scripting
audience, 56
"back to audience" (BTA), 49–50
beginnings, 53
breathing, 55
casting, 12, 41
Chamber Readers, 47–48, 60, 104
character narration, 41, 43
characters (in story or script), 41, 42, 54, 55
characters (readers and reading), 41, 42, 47, 49–50, 52, 54, 55
costumes, 9, 48
cuts and changes, 41, 42, 44
dialog, 41, 42, 43
directing, 47–56
endings, 53
entrances and exits, 48, 49–50
equipment, 48
eye movement, 49, 55
facial expression, 54
Floss, James, 60
focus, 47, 52
"freezes," 50, 53
illusions, 50, 52
Institute for Readers Theatre, 100, 104
introductions, 53
language arts, 9
memorization, 9, 49
mime, 47, 49, 50, 53, 101
modeling, 55
movement, 47, 48, 49–51, 54, 55
movement diagrams, 50, 51

music stands, 47
narration (in story and script), 9, 41, 42, 43
narrators (readers and reading), 41, 43, 47, 49, 50, 52, 53, 54, 55
oral interpretation. *See* reading (for reader's theater)
pauses, 54
performing, 56
placement and positioning, 43, 47, 49–50
posture, 55
props, 48, 49
reader's theater
    benefits, 9
    definition, 9, 40
    features, 40
    history, 9
    spellings, 9
    styles, 9, 47–48
    uses, 9
Readers Theatre Digest, 102
ReadersTheater (email list), 102
reading (general), 9, 42
reading (for reader's theater), 54–56
rehearsal, 49, 53, 54–55
role tags, 44
roles, 41, 55
RT. *See* reader's theater
scene changes, 49, 50, 54
scenes, 41, 42, 49
screens, folding, 48
script binders, 48
script format, 43–44, 45–46
script handling, 9, 47, 48–49, 53, 55
script marking, 54
scripts and scripting, 41–46

sets, 9, 49
smocks, 48
social studies, 9
sound effects, 50
stage directions, 42, 44, 54
staging, 9, 40, 47–53
stools, 47, 48, 49, 50
story selection, 41

tag lines, 42
team scripting, 44, 59
training, 58–60, 104
vocabulary, 42, 54
vocal exercises, 55
vocal expression, 42, 54, 55
Wagner, Jean, 47
Wilder, Thornton, 52

About the Author

Aaron Shepard is the award-winning author of numerous picture books as well as many stories in *Cricket* and other magazines. Between 1986 and 1991, he was a professional actor in Chamber Readers, a nonprofit reader's theater company that has performed since 1975 in the schools of Humboldt County, California. During his five years with the group, he scripted and directed many of its performance pieces and led workshops for teachers, librarians, and students. In 1986 and 1987, he also performed, scripted, and directed for Radio Readers on local public radio.

Aaron left professional reader's theater in 1991, when he moved away from Humboldt County. But in 1993 he published *Stories on Stage* (H. W. Wilson), considered by many the premier collection of reader's theater scripts.

Since 1994, Aaron has shared scripts on the Internet through his acclaimed series Reader's Theater Editions. First run as an email service, the series found its current home on the Web in 1996 as part of Aaron Shepard's RT Page (www.aaronshep.com/rt). This is today the Web's most popular reader's theater destination, with visits by thousands of teachers and librarians each week.

Aaron now lives in southern California.